MARKETING
Insights and
Outrages

Michael.

   I thought you might
like a bit of Outrage.

   All the best at Sense –
and beyond.

ALSO BY DRAYTON BIRD:

Commonsense Direct Marketing (3rd edn)

> 'So clear and concise that selective quotations fail to do justice to the richness of its texture. Read it.'
>
> Campaign

> 'Drayton Bird knows more about direct marketing than anyone in the world. His book is pure gold.'
>
> David Ogilvy

The most authoritative, and popular, European book on direct marketing ever published, offering practical, commonsense advice to both practitioners and students.

£18.99   Paperback   ISBN 0 7494 2584 9   384 pages

How to Write Sales Letters That Sell

> 'If you manage to take on board just half of the suggestions, you will never write a dud sales letter again.'
>
> Business Matters

Whatever is being sold – high or low price, product or service – the chances of a sales letter not being consigned to the waste basket will improve vastly if you follow this step-by-step advice.

£16.99   Paperback   ISBN 0 7494 1431 6   256 pages

Available from all good booksellers. For further information on these and other marketing titles, please contact:

Kogan Page
120 Pentonville Road
London N1 9JN
Tel: 020 7278 0433
Fax: 020 7837 6348
e-mail: kpinfo@kogan-page.co.uk

or visit our Web site: www.kogan-page.co.uk

MARKETING
Insights and Outrages

DRAYTON BIRD

A COLLECTION OF PITHY PIECES FROM
 Marketing MAGAZINE

KOGAN
PAGE

First published in 2000

Kogan Page Limited
120 Pentonville Road
London N1 9JN, UK

Kogan Page (US) Limited
163 Central Avenue, Suite 4
Dover, NH 03820, USA

© Drayton Bird, 2000

British Library Cataloguing in Publication Data

A CIP record for this book is available from the British Library.

ISBN 0 7494 3215 2

Typeset by Kogan Page Limited
Printed and bound in Great Britain by Clays Ltd, St Ives plc

CONTENTS

FOREWORD

In the world of marketing, obsessed as it is with the new, the different and the fashionable, it's rare to find a voice willing to point out that the emperor of the month is, in fact, stark bollock naked.

Drayton Bird is that voice. In five years of editing his columns for *Marketing*, I can honestly say there wasn't a single one that failed to worry me.

Sometimes it was because I feared he might have libelled someone with a fat bank balance and lawyers to match. Occasionally, it was because he would insist on promoting his latest book in his column and still expect us to pay him for it.

And now, here I am plugging Drayton's latest book, and very definitely not receiving a penny in return.

This means either that I've been beaten into submission by a couple of hundred columns and slightly fewer lunches, or that I'm happy to recommend this book because, despite all the grey hairs and nasty phone calls I've collected as a result of them, I think these columns are priceless.

Think of *Marketing Insights and Outrages* as a gymnasium for the marketing mind. The mental muscles you'll develop here are those of scepticism and common sense, both of which will need to be pumped up and bulging if you're to fight your way through the torrent of fads, trends and snake oil remedies that pass for insight in the world of advertising and promotion.

If you reckon you're sceptical enough already, then read them for no other reason that, whether or not you know the characters involved, you'll laugh out loud at least eight times while doing so, and there aren't many business books you can say that about.

Oh, and once you're addicted, you might like to turn to *Marketing* for your regular fix. There, done it. I've finally plugged my publication in one of Drayton's. Maybe I've learnt more from him than I thought.

Mike Hewitt, Publishing Director, Marketing

November 1999

WHAT THIS BOOK WILL DO FOR YOU

Every age has its little fads and fashions, but some, perhaps, have more serious consequences than others.

In the 20th century quite a few pretentious but dubious sciences or disciplines have emerged. We have benefited from psychology, psychiatry, sociology and their bastard offspring counselling – all too often prurience masquerading as benevolence – and economics, which even economists are rude about.

I doubt if marketers have caused as much misery as psychiatrists, who for so many years destroyed so many lives through the enthusiastic application of electric shocks and nowadays still regularly release murderous lunatics to rape and kill our children. Mind you, since we now know Dr Freud made up many of his case histories, this is hardly surprising.

I am not sure to what degree such sharp practice exists among marketers. I have seen a fair amount, but ill-founded conceit and stupidity seem to me more common than plain dishonesty. Nevertheless, it is very hard for ordinary folk, and even many practitioners, to make sense of some of the things that go on.

I imagine, for instance, if you made a list of skilled marketers you would place the names Coca-Cola and Pepsi Cola fairly near the top. Regularly in surveys of such trivia Coca-Cola is voted the world's top brand. And perhaps Hoover would deserve a place on your list. After all, there are not many human activities where one name becomes so pre-eminent that it is applied to an entire category. This came home to me when my PA, the radiant Denise, told me a while ago that she owned an Electrolux Hoover.

How, then, are we to explain away why on one occasion Coca-Cola decided, after who knows what extensive research and forethought by phalanxes of great minds, that they should reformulate and relaunch their sickly concoction as 'New' Coke? And for those interested in curiosities, how is it that however many people may have lost jobs as a result, the man who had this foolish idea was promoted to become marketing boss of the whole enterprise?

And what about their deadly rival, Pepsi Cola? Which genius there decided to spend $500 million or more changing the colour of its cans and thus reduce sales at a stroke by 5 per cent – a disaster that usually takes years of dedicated incompetence? I don't actually know how high the person who came up with this floperoo was promoted but no doubt that person is enjoying the fruits of this labour right now on a beach somewhere.

For that matter, examine the case of Hoover. Someone there had the stunning idea of offering free holidays to people who bought their machines. Since the value of the holidays appeared greater than the cost of the machines, the result – unsurprisingly, you would have thought – was that hordes of people bought machines to get the holidays. Perhaps even less surprisingly, Hoover couldn't supply them all. The final consequence of that little wheeze was no surprise either. The customers were all very angry; Hoover ended up going broke and in the end was bought by someone else.

This book is a collection of pieces I have written over the years which endeavours to explore and explain some of these little peculiarities. Why do people do such stupid things? What kind of people are they anyhow? And why do so many of them seem almost totally lacking in common sense or ability to learn? The answers are often as bewildering as they are hilarious.

I have a practical purpose, too. I have tried where possible to suggest things you ought not to do if you want your enterprise to flourish, and to encourage you to do those that experience shows will usually pay off better for you. It is a rather alarming reflection that if you plough through these pages diligently and make notes you will probably end up better informed than quite a number of marketers, too many of whom are little more than plausible idlers. (I speak from personal practice, you understand.)

At the insistence of my charming publisher, the book is divided into sections to make it appear organized. Please do not be deceived by this stratagem. As you will see, each of these pieces covers at least two subjects and some as many as five. However, to prevent being exposed as a fraud, I have tried to make sure that each contains some element, however fleeting, which justifies its being in the category.

I will end by saying that this is what they call good bedtime reading, ie there is no plot; just read two or three pieces at a time, and if they don't put you to sleep, ask for your money back.

BRIC-À-BRAC

Introduction

'A place for everything and everything in its place' is the sort of sententious statement I can imagine Mary Poppins delivering.

If you have read the introduction to this book you will recall that my publisher twisted my arm to make me organize the whole thing under what seem like logical sections. I'm not sure I will ever forgive her, since apart from anything else, this transformed what I originally conceived as an easy recycling job into something approaching a nightmare.

Well, these are the pieces that, try as I might, I couldn't fit into anything approaching a sensible category so I've called them bric-à-brac – random thoughts I come across in the attic I call my mind and feel compelled to pour out.

ANOTHER BLAST OF HOT AIR

That remarkable thinker Theodore Zeldin (1994) says an opportunity is wasted every time a meeting has taken place and nothing has happened. If so, most of us spend a depressingly high percentage of our lives on fruitless chatter.

This is often no accident, since many meetings are not intended to achieve anything, having been proposed for sundry selfish reasons. A common one, which also begets much market research, is the desire of an individual or individuals to avoid being responsible for a decision. This is often wise, since whilst it is perfectly possible that someone may be fired for getting something wrong, few firms are so callous or determined as to get rid of a whole group because of something for which no one person can be blamed.

> The greatest curse of meetings is that most produce nothing.

Some meetings have objectives so ludicrous it is inconceivable they can be achieved. Thus, about four years ago a client assembled about 16 people from all over the world in London to discuss nothing less than the complete restructuring of benefits and services his vast organization offered to its millions of customers. How he imagined the very basis of his firm's business could be transformed for the better by eight hours' jabbering around a conference table I did not understand. I spent most of the day trying to calculate the cost in air fares and fees of those present – who included, apart from the company's representatives and those of their agencies, some astoundingly expensive management consultants from the United States and Europe.

Many meetings revolve around presentations, but few receive the rapt attention they deserve. A few years ago a friend, Roger Millington, entered the wrong conference room at a big agency. He thought he was talking to an audience of people selling ladies' underwear, whereas they were from Goodyear Tyres. He swears he was a good 10 minutes into his spiel before anyone noticed everything he was saying was hilariously irrelevant.

When I first became a creative director many years ago I soon learnt meetings were an even greater theft of time than procrastination and never attended unless forced to, merely sending in advance my written views on the subject in question, offering to turn up and discuss them if asked. I don't recall this ever happening, which probably says more than I would like about the poor quality of my thinking. In *Up the Organisation*, Robert Townsend, who made Avis successful, suggests all meetings be held standing up so people will not dawdle.

But Zeldin is right. The greatest curse of meetings is that most produce nothing. Either there is no conclusion save that another meeting should take place or, if it is decided what should be done, it is not made clear by whom; and even if that essential point is established, it is rarely made clear by when it must be done.

If what I have written reflects your own experience, I am not at all surprised. But if your organization does not suffer from these vices, it either already is or soon will be amazingly successful. But don't get complacent. Given enough meetings, it won't stay that way long.

□ □ □

DATE: JUNE 1996

CONFUSED? YOU WILL BE

Have you been following, as I have, the thrilling adventures of 'Big Ed' Carter, who has been brought over from the United States by BT to introduce their Friends and Family programme? For the life of me I can't think why; the idea started in the United States with another firm he worked for. Why didn't someone from BT go over, study it and just knock it off? It's not that complicated. They're too lazy, I suppose.

Carter is 1.9 metres tall. Suppose he were like a certain type of US citizen – as vast in girth as height. He would be a very barrage balloon of blubber – overweight, overpaid and over here, to adapt the old line. Maybe he's lean, lithe and magnificent, but one thing is for sure: he has quite a name for thuggish behaviour – his physical violence caused BT's agency, AMV-BBDO, to ban him from their premises. We should salute them; it takes courage to do that to somebody influential at the country's biggest advertiser, whereas it takes very little to thump people if you're built like a Sherman tank.

> **A**re the talents needed to rise to the top in these huge firms those required to run them?

They have now reaffirmed the ban, because another of their clients, Simon Esberger of Cellnet, has hired Carter to start a Friends and Family type programme and help them 'escape the industry's looming price war'. This may be a good idea, even if it's a shame he can't get somebody house-trained to do it, but the logic escapes me. Joking apart, friends, what would you call a scheme whereby you pay less when you ring several specified numbers? In Ashton-under-Lyne where I was brought up, folk would say it is about price. In fact even in London, where they like to complicate things a little, I imagine most people would say it is price-led. So what is Mr Esberger talking about, or to be more exact what is he talking through?

Here's something else I can't quite get my head round. Lloyds Bank-TSB is getting out of estate agency. Ten years and God knows how many millions (billions?) later they've decided it was all a bad idea and are looking for a management buy-out. But was the idea so bad? A network of financial service firms cross-selling to each other makes perfect sense. I suspect not enough thought was applied to the boring details. You have to ensure every likely relevant opportunity is exploited and every appropriate communication sent.

These people think strategies execute themselves. When they fail to do so, the solution applied often puzzles me. They squander shareholders' money to buy some firm for more than it's worth. Lots of people lose their jobs – 'economies of scale'. Things go wrong. Then the very people they employed – who failed – borrow the money to buy the firm back and end up making millions each. Why couldn't they do it before? Maybe they were just badly managed.

Are the talents needed to rise to the top in these huge firms those required to run them? And why do these precious economies of scale never reach as far as the top?

NOTE: You will learn more about the life and times of Big Ed Carter on page 82. Mr Esberger, who became famous for approving a very good advertising campaign for Häagen-Dazs ice-cream, did not last long at Cellnet. But why should selling ice-cream qualify you to sell phones, I wonder?

□ □ □

DATE: FEBRUARY 1998

10

DUBIOUS LOGIC; WRONG CONCLUSIONS

'Long live the Church of England, and down with enthusiasm,' cried an 18th-century bishop when blessing a set of church bells due to go to South Seas missionaries.

He was attacking the enthusiasm of dissenters. But the older I get the more I incline to the good bishop's thinking – and never more than when reading Andy Blackford on 6 October 1994 in the columns of *Marketing*, writing in praise of direct and promotional marketing. In the process he dismissed advertising as irrelevant nowadays. I got the impression he regards it as something like a confidence trick, which a new breed of intelligent consumers has seen through.

> **E**ven direct marketers benefit from illogical consumers who think buying directly is a better deal than buying through normal channels.

I wonder whether he knows what he's talking about. He appears to suggest advertising came about as a result of mass production. Whilst **mass** advertising was facilitated by technology, and particularly steam printing, advertising itself has been around much longer. Indeed, around the time the bishop was damning enthusiasm, Dr Johnson suggested advertising was so near perfect it was beyond improvement.

He assumes that after hundreds of years of being illogical about brands, consumers have suddenly become rational, and from now on will only **buy** products offering 'real measurable qualities with real measurable benefits'.

In the 18th century they believed briefly in the concept of enlightenment, but who really thinks human beings are any more enlightened now than they were?

They are certainly no better educated. Most know more of astrology than logic; few read anything other than tripe. A mere glance at what is going on in Bosnia and elsewhere suggests people remain as they ever were, infinitely more swayed by emotion than reason.

What impartial evidence suggests people are less willing now than 30 years ago to pay a premium for a brand, even though the product is almost impossible to distinguish from its competition? Does Andy Blackford really believe Tango, Gold Blend or Boddingtons succeeded because of rational consumers? Advertising, mass advertising, appealing almost entirely to emotions and certainly not intellect, did the trick – and always will – especially for this type of product.

'Precision techniques will sell better than advertising,' suggests Mr Blackford. Only sometimes. There will never be a better way of conveying a simple message to large numbers at a low cost than advertising; and when even a cheap mailing pack costs about 50p to reach one person, direct mail will never be an economical way to reach all your prospects.

Even direct marketers benefit from illogical consumers who think buying directly is a better deal than buying through normal channels. A recent survey of insurance policies in a Sunday paper showed that traditional channels often offer a better deal – despite which increasing numbers of consumers (and insurers) are moving towards the direct route.

People believe what they want to believe, including the idea that an advertised product in some mysterious way is better than an unadvertised one – which is why people like Procter & Gamble spend billions every year on building brands. They know that on average advertised brands are more profitable than those that aren't. This is not going to change, any more than consumers will.

□ □ □

DATE: OCTOBER 1994

HAUTE HOGWASH

One of my Sydney colleagues was 'swooped by a maggie' last month, pecked in the eye and nearly lost his sight. It seems the indigenous magpie violently attacks anyone who approaches the nest at mating time. Malcolm Auld, my partner there, claims country kids walk to school wearing plastic ice-cream containers to protect themselves – a grand new use for old packaging.

It's been a year for catastrophe in Oz. New improved myxomatosis, a viral disease that slays rabbits much faster than the original, is raging. Apparently a journo visiting a quarantine station left not merely with the usual pile of clichés but also the virus. It has killed so many bunnies that the skins to make those wacky hats festooned with beer cans, corks, ping-pong balls or anything to keep the flies off are so scarce they're having to import them from the UK.

> Technique and content matter infinitely less than the ability of critics to write hogwash about it.

In addition the fruit fly has swept in from the Pacific islands, to be greeted with less than total joy in northern Queensland where it's devastated the mango industry. Meanwhile the bogong – a moth about the size of a small plane – has been blown by strong winds to Sydney, where it does a lot more than get up people's noses, being found in beds, air vents and air-conditioning units. Like all moths it loves lights and so has brought a new look to the harbour bridge at night. The birds love the situation and hunt moths happily through the hours of darkness.

One plague, though, is worldwide: haute piffle from the moguls of the rag trade. On a plane flight I was mesmerized by some magazine interviews with Calvin Klein, Ralph Lauren and Donna Karan, who boldly went where no poser has gone before. Ralph Lauren believes, 'A sensibility now is the freedom of breaking the rules. Sensing the thrust of it [sic] out there. There's a heritage behind my designs, but there's also a newness and excitement that I inject.' Calvin Klein in his ads tries, would you believe, to 'create an image of what the product is'. He asks, 'Who am I attracting? Who do I think will wear this? Who will understand it? But then the photograph has to say something to me that's emotional. It has to make my heart start beating.' Donna Karan, though, delivers a quality of blather that leaves the other two in the dressing room. Success has been **such** a strain for her, poor lamb: 'People don't realize the demands and how difficult this job is. In every creation, there's the responsibility of that creation... I became a statistic of what was happening out there. Now I feel this power and I can try to shift it in my own moral way. I can try to work on developing a consciousness between my own ability and the people around me – the industry, the public. And I really do believe that is my mission.'

In *The Painted Word* (reprinted 1999), Tom Wolfe pointed out why much modern art is crap: technique and content matter infinitely less than the ability of critics to write hogwash about it. These fashion bozos go one better. They produce their own hogwash.

NOTE: You can read more about my friend Malcolm Auld and his adventures on pages 157–58.

□ □ □

DATE: DECEMBER 1995

HYPOCRISY AND LOGIC EXAMINED

'How is it that the loudest yelps for freedom come from the drivers of negroes?' asked Dr Johnson before the American War of Independence. Similarly, I sometimes wonder by what coincidence our two most xenophobic ministers – Howard and Portillo – are born of foreign parents. Could their minds have been unhinged by a surfeit of *Sun* editorials?

Five weeks ago I saw an article suggesting Howard is disliked because of his looks. His mind worries me more. I am even told his proposed immigration laws would have excluded his own parents from coming here before the war. Being Jewish they would have been in danger of their lives – though to look on the bright side we would have been spared him.

In Washington, DC guns are rife and deaths by shooting particularly common. You might even think that since a significant percentage of the victims are children something would be done about it.

Another politician with no sense of irony is Joseph Kennedy (Democrat, Massachusetts), now waging a campaign to restrict US booze advertising. How did young Joe arrive in his present situation – stinking rich and pontificating to everyone from his representative's pulpit? Largely because his grandfather, the villainous pro-Nazi Joe, made such a pile out of bootlegging during prohibition that he could buy his son John F the US presidency.

His proposal and others like it have always been rejected by the US Supreme Court because they restrict the freedom of speech: advertising informs people, however slightly, about things they might not otherwise hear about; and if it is legal to buy and sell, it should be legal to advertise. How sad that US politicians fool about with such trivia, yet have failed to control the one factor which clearly causes infinitely more misery: guns. Is it that hard to understand that people who own guns are going to shoot them, and as a consequence other people are going to get killed?

Surely, even for politicians, that can't be too difficult to work out. In Washington, DC, guns are rife and deaths by shooting particularly common. You might even think that since a significant percentage of the victims are children something would be done about it – but how much easier to squabble about whether homosexuals should marry or join the military than fight the National Rifle Association. I say this with some heat, since two young members of my American wife's family have died violently in the past five years.

And what about us? Soon we shall have a Labour Government, swiftly followed by an avalanche of regulations to make sure we behave as our betters think fit. To be fair this is already prevalent in the present government – the Bottomley tendency: 'We know better than you how to run your life.'

There will be further restrictions on advertising things that do us harm, starting with tobacco and moving on to alcohol. The logic is crazy. Why not outlaw ads for crisps, hamburgers, fish and chips, sausages, beef, lamb, eggs, cheese, cream, fried chicken and biscuits – in fact, anything that can harm you? Why not ban advertising for cars, oil, petrol and tyres – all those commercials of people racing along, their hair blowing freely in the breeze? After all, people die in road accidents. On this basis, crossing the road should be banned. Nonsense. But dangerous nonsense, if you believe in freedom.

NOTE: Many of the things I predicted have come to pass, though there have been one or two surprises.

The present government has indeed buried us under a landslide of busybody legislation. Happily, one of my clients publishes it all, and people have to read it whether they want to or not.

Mr Portillo, realizing his views were not getting him ahead, has abandoned them with the alacrity of a true politician to become a gentler, kinder person, besides admitting to youthful homosexual adventures.

☐ ☐ ☐

DATE: JULY 1996

INCOMPETENCE (AND INCONTINENCE) ON EVERY SIDE

Last night I had a terrible fright. I was directing a thin yellow trickle against the wall of a garage next to Bridgwater railway station when a concerned citizen came to check if I was a burglar. 'Not at all,' I explained. 'It's just that I can't use the station toilet.'

A little notice within the station booking-hall reads – literally: 'Toilets close at 14.30 hours (2.30 pm). As agreed by the station manager.' This rare blend of illiteracy, arrogance and incompetence swiftly called to mind the pungent aroma of recycled tripe that has been fouling the air lately, emanating for the most part from Blackpool and Brighton.

Which party should we disdain more: the Blairites, who promise more

> The problem our politicians face is simple. They deal in two commodities, both in almost limitless supply: hot air, and other people's money. So they think if they talk loud enough and spend prodigally enough it will solve any problem.

money for hospitals, for schools (and God knows they'll need it with all the free computers), for pensioners and better public services, without giving us the vaguest clue as to how these goodies are to be paid for; or the Conservatives, featuring such as Michael Howard, face oozing deceit from every pore, who says he will lock up all wrongdoers for longer than ever before, without the slightest regard for the fact that first you have to catch them? The average burglar, it seems, has only one chance in seven of being caught, so **any** sentence – long or short – is irrelevant.

Somebody pointed out last week that part of Mr Blair's speech was copied from the amphibian, or rather reptilian, Gingrich (who also promises a kiddies' computer bonanza) and part from that great statesman, Harold

Wilson. But the mendacity displayed by both parties reminds me of nothing so much as the splendid election campaign in the 18th century that was won on the slogan of 'Give us back our eleven days' – a poignant appeal referring to some trifling but necessary changes in the calendar. Of course, in those days most voters were either drunk or illiterate, or both – which, come to think of it, probably applies to our present electorate equally well. But at least they used to insist on being bribed in real money, not phoney promises.

The problem our politicians face is simple. They deal in two commodities, both in almost limitless supply: hot air, and other people's money. So they think if they talk loud enough and spend prodigally enough it will solve any problem. But money is useless without intelligent planning. The result is bad service on every side. Thus, a seven-figure sum has been spent in renovating Bridgwater station. The perfectly serviceable 19th-century toilets have been closed, with new ones placed in the booking hall, which is locked promptly at 2.30 every day. Nobody has given any thought to the consequences of this for the aged and incontinent, like me. Or consider the Post Office. A century ago you could post a letter in the centre of London before lunch to tell your wife in the suburbs you would not be arriving back for dinner, in the confident knowledge it would get there. Not now!

What it all adds up to is that, whereas politicians are getting ever more subtle in their gradations of bullshit, none of them could run a brothel on a troop train.

NOTE: Newt Gingrich, a creepy Republican politician now discredited, suggested giving computers to all US schools, an idea copied by Tony Blair, a creepy Labour politician not yet discredited.

I discuss the sorrows of Bridgwater station in another piece – and the perils of believing politicians in several. Having worked for the Tories under Thatcher and Major, and then for Labour under Blair, I feel thoroughly ashamed of myself.

□ □ □

DATE: OCTOBER 1995

PHONEY SOLUTIONS

When the business history of our times is written, if anyone can be bothered, a good title would be *The Era of Quack Nostrums*. Benchmarking, down-sizing, right-sizing, re-engineering, JIT, TQM: buzzwords and initials are coined as fast as business theorists can bang out pretentious, often incomprehensible tomes to justify them.

I have seen a fair number of these patent remedies applied, and the consequences – which are usually devastating, especially to the poor staff. One of my clients, a huge multinational, even appointed a head of re-engineering. I met a friend who had just had a meeting with him. When he said her department was going to be right-sized, she responded that it sounded very like a good old-fashioned mass firing to her – which of course it was.

> **Personally, I learn most from people who do things rather than talk about them.**

In one article I read how Mercury hired some consultants with disastrous results, ending with a giant 'motivational' rally where their staff were confused and upset by having a barrage of multi-syllabic tripe, which no doubt cost a fortune to think up, bellowed at them.

Too many of these patent solutions, I fear, are applied by senior managers unwilling to look in the mirror and recognize their own incompetence, an incompetence often matched, I have found, by that of the business witch-doctors themselves. I was once invited to join a meeting of international TQM consultants. When I wrote to them all afterwards, not one was competent enough to respond. In one case I introduced a multi-million-dollar prospective client. The quality 'guru' in question didn't even get round to contacting him.

Even intelligent people are taken in by these moon-gazers. The regional boss of one big advertising network hired one to address an international conference he had arranged at vast expense. Two participants showed me a wondrous chart he had created, with lines, arrows and dashes going hither and yon, rather like an electrical circuit diagram. They were most impressed, though unable to reply intelligently when I asked: 'As a result of this chart what precisely are you going to do differently tomorrow from what you do today?'

Personally, I learn most from people who do things rather than talk about them. Last year I stayed at a hotel with levels of service I have only encountered at a handful of others around the world. I asked the manager what magic potion he had applied. It had no initial, and few syllables. He said, 'I don't believe in theories and rule-books. I simply tell people, "When you're dealing with a customer, ask yourself: if you were that customer, what would **you** like? It will probably be what they would like; and what's more it will probably be what I as a manager would like."'

I recommend this simple approach, which works admirably for that hotel, and certainly would for your business. There is, of course, a fancy phrase for it – 'staff empowerment' – and no doubt someone has written a needlessly long and dreary book about it; but when I was young the expression was 'Do unto others as you would be done by' – not a bad maxim, and you don't need a book to understand it.

NOTE: The hotel I mention is The Observatory in Sydney.

Mercury was a phone company launched to compete with British Telecom. Their advertising, which was very funny, won buckets of awards. Their advertising agency became famous and successful. They never made money because their advertising was more interesting than their proposition. Now they are called something else.

□ □ □

DATE: FEBRUARY 1996

THE ARROGANCE OF DO-GOODERS

Did you read about the latest great idea from the busybodies at the NSPCC? They think children should be discouraged from kissing their grandparents. Maybe they should change their name to the NSPAC – the National Society to Prohibit Affectionate Children.

It seems they think such affection may lead to perversion; and their boss, a self-righteous freak called Harding, actually defends this. I'm puzzled. What would he say if he knew I still kiss my (now adult) sons, and smother my grandchildren with kisses? What does this make me? An incestuous paedophile? Or a dreadful old queen? (Mind you, that would probably make me a beneficiary of today's political correctness.)

> **P**hil just *loved* the idea of going down in the school files as a suspected child abuser.

Of course, this is the man who launched the utterly bogus campaign to end all child abuse in a couple of years. How can you completely extirpate any such wickedness – let alone that quickly? Such dishonesty strengthens my suspicion that an alarmingly high percentage of charity marketers are a) round the twist and b) happy to make any promise, no matter how wild, to get money. A good parallel is our glorious Government's promises on schools, hospitals, transport, ethical arms policy, sleaze – you name it.

But my feelings are nothing compared to those of my partner, Phil Brisk. Years ago he wrote copy that said, 'If you suspect a child is being mistreated, call the NSPCC.' This proved a licence for mayhem. Phil and his wife have themselves twice been victims of cruel, false (and, thank God, easily disproved) allegations of cruelty to their children, bringing the police to their door.

After great effort, Phil got through to an NSPCC apparatchik and asked why they don't insist complainants give their names in exchange for an assurance they won't be passed on. Other agencies do this to discourage hoax callers. This means they can report back to complainants, reassure them if their worries are groundless and maybe clear some poor innocent bastard's name in the process.

The NSPCC man didn't want to know. He thought their present methods were just fine. Yes, innocent parents would sometimes get hurt; but set against cruelty to children, what a small price to pay. Phil really hit the roof, though, when he was told not to worry. Not only had the police given his wife and himself a glowing report, but so had their health visitor and the headmistress of the school their eldest son was **due** to start at a month later. Unbelievable. Having got the police report on the Saturday, these holier-than-thou twats were still going through their 'standard investigative procedure' on the Monday. Phil just **loved** the idea of going down in the school files as a suspected child abuser.

Phil said to me, with his customary subtle use of language, 'I'll never leave those bastards a penny in my will.' And for my part, I wondered whether I should have taken a table at an event that helped raise a lot of money for them. Cruelty to children is evil. But there's another evil: the creation of a climate where children are raised to become unreasonably scared and suspicious of adults – and adults too become scared, rightly, that one day they'll be the victims of calumny.

The NSPCC, with their arrogant, end-always-justifies-the-means attitudes, have a lot to answer for.

NOTE: In all fairness, this campaign has proved outstandingly successful. Do the ends justify the means? I wonder.

□ □ □

DATE: AUGUST 1999

TIME FOR A NEW APPROACH FROM AGENTS?

My dentist makes a small fortune out of putting sundry ingenious pieces of miniature architecture in my mouth, which I plan to leave eventually to the Natural History Museum as an example of what can be achieved by a determined practitioner who gets his hands on a customer with more money than teeth.

Our sado-masochistic relationship allows me plenty of time to flip through sundry glossy magazines, from one of which, *Marie Claire*, I recently learnt that Christina Appelt, 41, runs a dating agency in Berlin for married folk who want to screw around. It seems she is doing very well. Among the secrets of her success she emphasizes the importance of vetting people carefully. For instance, it seems that her clients are not that keen on boffing foreigners – not that Berliners are racist, she adds swiftly – and she takes care to weed out people with eccentric tastes.

> **M**any of those who act as agents are seen not as intelligent, worthy contributors to society, but rather as opportunistic leeches.

'I have an instinct for these things,' she said modestly. She gave as an example of her uncanny skill 'the man who came in a few weeks ago dressed from top to toe in rubber'. I think you'd have to be as thick as two short planks not to suspect that someone who goes in search of sexual adventures dressed as a frogman has something a wee bit special in mind, but we'll let that pass.

Having spent years as an agent myself, I have great sympathy for anyone who fulfils this difficult role. Many of those who act as agents are seen not as intelligent, worthy contributors to society, but rather as opportunistic leeches. Think of all the show-business stories about agents, or the way people view estate agents: for years I have used a joke about them as an example of all-round shiftiness in my speeches, and rarely failed to raise a laugh. Which brings us to the subject of advertising agents, and why, as recent reports have it, clients are turning less and less to them for advice on strategy – whatever that may be.

Is this because they think agency people lack intelligence – or they don't trust agencies as much as they did? Could it be they sometimes fear there may be some slight relationship between profit and the eagerness with which agencies urge them to invest in expensive TV campaigns and very big newspaper spaces with remarkably few words inside them? I fear these unworthy thoughts may well lurk in the odd breast. Indeed, one has only to look at the rise of the media independents and the regular howls of anguish about TV production costs to confirm it.

There is an interesting parallel in another agency business. The airlines are fast moving to cut out the travel agent and go direct to customers. This is quite a familiar situation in business today and rather like what clients are doing when they go direct to media independents rather than through their agencies. The solution some travel agents have found is instructive. It is quite simply to do what they should have been doing all the time: act as helpful advisers to the customer rather than as vendors for the airlines and holiday companies. In other words they are becoming increasingly involved in managing people's travel expenditures and making sure they get the best deal.

'Tell your client to do what you would if you were in his place,' said David Ogilvy. How many do, I wonder?

□ □ □

DATE: JANUARY 1997

WHAT MAKES RICHARD RUN?

A few years ago I read in a survey of American millionaires that most managed their personal finances hopelessly. If you knew my skills in that area as well as my bank, you would realize why I found this so heartening. It encouraged me to keep trying.

However, I still find finance hard work and most writing on the subject as clear as mud, which is why I was delighted last week to find in a paper called the *New York Guardian* not one, but several, writers who were not only comprehensible but also entertaining. One did a rather sardonic analysis of the Donna Karan firm's share price suggesting the firm's high inventory and receivables make the shares very overrated, one reason being that their principal asset – the brand name – has been cunningly retained by Ms Karan and her husband.

> How does Virgin succeed in business after business – most seemingly unrelated? What makes Richard run? First, he knows a good new idea is the most powerful thing in marketing, so he'll listen to anyone who might have one.

This got me thinking about the value of a brand. Years ago most brands were associated with one thing, limiting the likely appeal of new products sold under the brand name. Take two famous brand associations: Bass means beer; Guinness means stout. I doubt if Bass could market a stout well under their name; Guinness has tried selling beer at least once – but not that successfully.

This changed rather surprisingly. To explain what I mean, would you believe a motorbike firm like BSA, Triumph or Harley–Davidson would do well at selling cars, let alone musical instruments? But Honda sell cars and marine engines successfully. Yamaha sell pianos, guitars and so forth. Is this because instead of being known for one product these firms became known for a desirable characteristic – in this case, quality?

But if that sort of thing is a bit of a stretch, what do you make of Richard Branson? Some time ago I wrote a rude column about a mailing sent out under the aegis of Virgin airlines. I then had to go to Australia. When I arrived my son rang me in a state of some excitement: 'Richard Branson has just rung to talk about the article you wrote. He's left his private number so you can ring him back.' Alas, Richard never became my best friend, but I have spent some time reflecting on him. Over two years ago I explained to an audience of financial marketers why I was sure his new financial venture – which many questioned – would do well. How does Virgin succeed in business after business – most seemingly unrelated? What makes Richard run?

First, he knows a good new idea is the most powerful thing in marketing, so he'll listen to anyone who might have one. Second, he has a simple competitive proposition: when you buy this, you are dealing with me, not some dull, grey, impersonal company. I have no idea what he's really like, but he personifies the brand, and labours tirelessly to project himself and what he stands for. And that is not a particular product, but a range of characteristics: service, quality, warmth, honesty, youth. Hard to beat if you work as hard as he does to deliver them.

NOTE: Richard Branson sent me a note thanking me for this piece. He must never sleep. Someone else wrote a letter to *Marketing* pointing out that BSA were originally arms manufacturers. Hmmm.

□ □ □

DATE: JANUARY 1997

WHY DON'T MARKETING DIRECTORS LAST VERY LONG?

Are you a marketing director? I don't envy you. Lately a client who reads *Campaign* regularly commented to me on a change. Where he used to see stories about accounts changing hands, now he sees more about people like you changing jobs.

They say the average tenure is now 15 months, or even less. Why? Do you all get bored quickly? Are most marketing directors so hopeless? Is the job too hard? Or are most firms such dreadful employers? Let's explore the possibilities.

Certainly you don't have much chance to achieve anything. By the time your 'vision' is implemented (you need a vision now; ideas are not enough), someone else has your job. And you can be sure they'll confuse change with improvement and alter everything.

> **B**y the time your 'vision' is implemented (you need a vision now; ideas are not enough), someone else has your job.

But you shouldn't have gone. The people who hired you should. Most of them must be criminally bad at perhaps the most vital job in business: finding and keeping good people. If I hired so poorly, so consistently, I'd have gone broke years ago.

There's good news if you have the right credentials, though. 'A growing number of marketers are being wooed by other sectors hungry for staff with FMCG experience,' said this journal two weeks ago. I hope they get the right ones, but the evidence is not promising. The last great wave of migration was after the financial world fell in love with marketing. Like most lovers they skimped on reconnaissance. 'What **is** marketing?' the bosses asked; so their gophers went to the odd seminar, read some books and articles and bought a few lunches. 'It's all about brands,' they said. 'Who knows about brands?' 'Those chaps who sell detergent,' was the answer.

Then the one thing these firms have plenty of was applied to the problem. It is called other people's money. And we all know what happened next. Most of it went down the drain, because neither they nor most of those they imported asked one or two dull but relevant questions. Like, 'Shouldn't we learn a bit about marketing before entrusting it to this chap from Mars Petfoods?' And, 'Do people buy insurance the way they buy crisps?'

What's really sad is that some of these people still haven't worked it out. Maybe trivia can be sold with puns and slogans – or 'straplines' as we now call them – but serious things can't. We work too hard for our money to joke about it. My pension is not trivial to me. My mortgage is not a fitting subject for fledgling wit. It pays for my home. Fifty snappy words from a 23-year-old copywriter won't get me to switch my bank account. Nor will such frippery sell legal services, computers, or accountancy well.

Of course, now and then someone does dream up a simple line that strikes to the heart of something. But it rarely comes from a big ad agency. There's a small firm of south London lawyers called Preuveneers. On their building a sign says, 'One day you will need a lawyer. When you do, we'll be here.' I wish I'd thought of that.

NOTE: Life is full of disappointments. Someone I know went to Preuveneers. Their service was so bad she would sue them – if only she could find a lawyer who would help.

☐ ☐ ☐

DATE: JUNE 1998

JUNK

Introduction

It's funny how life turns out.

After 20-odd years toiling away at all sorts of things – journalism, advertising, selling swimming pools, publishing, franchising, even, as I recall on page 191, selling whisky over the phone – I finally succeeded as a junk-mail king.

Why are direct mail and direct marketing (the two are often seen as the same) so particularly singled out as junk? As I point out in another piece, many kinds of junk disfigure our lives.

The reason, when you think about it, is pretty obvious. In the late 70s marketers began to spend a lot of money on mail. It took no time for the other media to work out that they would not be spending that money with them. No wonder then, that those who hate direct mail and direct marketing most are the other media.

They have done such an excellent job of running it down that direct marketers feel downright sorry for themselves, poor lambs. Several times the great and good of the industry have suggested competitions and campaigns to find a new name for junk mail and persuade people to use it.

It would never work, because the public does what it pleases. But if you are interested in the thinking – or lack of it – behind the stuff that slips through your letterbox or appears in your papers and on your screens asking you to reply now, here are some observations from somebody who has been blamed more than most for it.

AN INFALLIBLE GUIDE TO GOOD ADVERTISING

From time to time people at parties accuse me of cynicism. I happily plead guilty, reminding them of the greatest cynic, Jesus Christ, who said, 'He that is without sin among you, let him first cast a stone' when the adulteress was about to be stoned to death.

A wise cynic once asked the United States' top creative directors which ads they most admired – then checked to see what sales they got. As you know, working out what sales advertising produces is so hard, many have despaired that it could ever be done, so I wonder how he measured this. However I do remember the ads the creative directors liked were amazingly bad when it came to making money.

> **I do remember the ads the creative directors liked were amazingly bad when it came to making money... If advertising and marketing pundits like it, disaster is highly likely – and vice versa.**

I have found this an admirable guide over the years. If advertising and marketing pundits like it, disaster is highly likely – and vice versa. For example, the experts cast scorn on the Goldfish card. What on earth has gas to do with financial services? Indeed, what on earth have goldfish got to do with them? It seemed such a zany idea that few believed it could work. So last week I read the crazy Goldfish already has over 500,000 admirers.

Compare this with the admiration showered on First Direct. After over eight years it hasn't done that much better than Goldfish in terms of customers. A friend in banking told me it has yet to turn a profit. Hard to believe – but even if it has, it took a hell of a long time. And how about 'The future is Orange' – the smuggest advertising campaign ever? Again, much praised – but not much to write home about if you're interested in profit.

I confess (for I too suffer from the curse of being a marketing man) I was sceptical about the Goldfish venture, though I know Bruce Rayner, who was involved, is pretty bright, with an agreeable touch of craziness. It's nice to be right occasionally, though. I said First Direct was vastly overrated years ago. The experts derided Branson's move into financial services. I predicted it would succeed. I also said the RAC rebranding jaunt would end in tears.

A few years ago I was conducting a seminar for some Unilever brand managers and assorted marketing functionaries – as self-satisfied a group of know-alls as you'll ever meet. One leant back languidly: 'Direct mail is all rubbish', he said. 'I get tons of it and throw it all away.'

'Extremely interesting – and profoundly irrelevant,' I replied. 'You'd have to go on a long hard fast day's drive across this country to find any group of people less like their customers than you lot. You spend your time in smart restaurants, talking about the minutiae of marketing plans. They think about important things, like whether their dog has to go to the vet, or who's going to win the World Cup.'

The plain fact is, most marketers are abysmally bad at understanding real people. As soon as they succeed they stop living real lives. They are corrupted; they end up appealing to their colleagues, not their customers.

NOTE: Nobody knows whether the Goldfish credit card is profitable yet. First Direct is a direct banker. Orange sell mobile telephony. When, after years of pretentious advertising, they started telling people what made them better, they began to do well. The RAC spent a monstrous amount of money changing their 'corporate identity' – jargon for the way they present themselves visually – but continued to do badly.

☐ ☐ ☐

DATE: JANUARY 1998

ANOTHER BUSINESS SCHOOL

A few years ago someone at Ogilvy & Mather asked their wonderful founder what constituted the ideal client. In response to this he came up with one of his famous lists. Point three said the client 'directs the agency to increase sales this quarter and to build an indestructible brand image for the long term. (Damn difficult to do in the same campaign.)'.

I was reminded of this when reading a revealing interview published a while ago in *Marketing* with 'the UK's latest marketing heavyweight, John Quelch, ex-professor of marketing at Harvard Business School and now in the hot seat as principal of the London Business School (LBS)'. The good Professor Quelch is very famous and successful, though every time I hear his name I can't help laughing. This isn't his fault. It's just that when I was at school, we all read a comic strip (Billy Bunter, I think) that featured a silly headmaster called Quelch.

> **Has he been locked in a Harvard toilet for the last 10 years? Direct marketing has built plenty of brands, like Direct Line, Goldfish, Lands' End, L L Bean, Viking, First Direct and MBNA.**

It appears this new Quelch is a bit of a comedian, too. He said, in the usual pompous way these business-school grandees try to impress the foolish: 'Excessive emphasis on productivity measures induce [which sounds ungrammatical, incidentally] a greater emphasis on direct marketing or short-term sales promotion activity at the expense of long-term investment in franchise-building activity.' He says he is 'distinctly wary' of shifting expenditure 'below the line' to disciplines like sales promotion and direct marketing.

How sweet that LBS has chosen a marketing Neanderthal as their new boss. What on earth makes him lump sales promotion and direct marketing together? And why on earth does he suppose direct marketing can't build a 'franchise'? Has he been locked in a Harvard toilet for the last 10 years?

Direct marketing has built plenty of brands, like Direct Line, Goldfish, Lands' End, L L Bean, Viking, First Direct and MBNA. Paradoxically, Quelch talked up the Internet and electronic commerce. If he ever logs on, he will notice all Internet commerce is direct. And maybe a kindly friend should tell him the entire economic basis of direct marketing is long term: planning starts with estimating the value of a customer over time, rather than the value of a sale. Surely he must have seen this concept mentioned by Peter Drucker before being stolen by his old colleague Theodore Levitt.

Quelch has advised 30 companies in the Fortune 500, and co-authored ('authored' is a US word for 'written') no end of books. He is a director of several big firms. I wonder if he has ever risked his own money in a business. Those who do swiftly adapt theory to reality. For instance, advertising agents rarely suggest direct marketing to their clients but they nearly all use (bad) direct mail and direct response ads to sell themselves.

Even *Advertising Age* has just banned the dopey phrase 'below the line' from its pages – seven years and three months after I condemned it in my first piece for this magazine. Are we so short of half-baked academics that we have to import other people's leftovers?

□ □ □

DATE: AUGUST 1998

DIRECT MAIL FOLLIES

Did you see the pictures of the man who organized President Clinton's election campaign – the one whose chilling ferocity of expression makes the average pit-bull terrier look like a lap-dog? Apparently he had pinned up on the wall of his campaign headquarters the line: 'It's the economy, stupid.'

I think the equivalent for direct marketers should be: 'It's targeting, dumbo,' a view reinforced when I re-read the other day that splendid book *Dear Personalised* (1992) by Tom Rayfield of JWT Direct.

This hero commented on every mailing his family received over a year, and since he is a prosperous JWT director, they received far more than the average – 530 in all. I salute his stoic endeavour.

Thoughtfully, he placed his conclusions at the start of the book for the benefit of idle and impatient souls like me, who immediately turn to the end of detective stories to find out whodunit. Almost everything he said was about targeting, which is much more important than the words and pictures, even if rather less interesting to work on. Here are 11 examples:

> '**A** bank wrote to my 13-year-old son about financial planning and a travel company sent him a free wine offer… he may be getting cynical about direct mail at an early age.'

1. Thirty-six per cent of the mailshots had his name and/or address significantly wrong – though he carefully gave them accurately.
2. He and his wife received identical mailshots in the same post with monotonous frequency.
3. A slight variation on this wasteful technique is to mail the same person twice. This also happened often.
4. 'Several mailshots were carefully personalized to the family who left our house nearly six years ago.'
5. 'Sending the identical mailshot five times to the same house over a period of four weeks – as at least one mailshotter did – begins to reduce the effectiveness of the words "your last chance".'

6. (My favourite example, perhaps.) The firm who sent him lots of beautiful brochures – all written in Norwegian.
7. (But I quite liked this too.) 'A bank wrote to my 13-year-old son about financial planning and a travel company sent him a free wine offer… he may be getting cynical about direct mail at an early age.'
8. The same company mails you from different departments and sometimes knows your name and birth date, and then forgets completely.
9. A company gives the name of a local dealer or where to go to a presentation – several hours' drive from your home.
10. The mailshotter gets his timing completely wrong. 'January is the least likely month to sell books. More are sold in the shops in December than at any other time.'
11. 'I have spent thousands of pounds with Thomas Cook and Austin Reed, but you wouldn't know it from their mailshots.'

Tom had other interesting comments on: cheap mailings from companies who should not appear cheap; the need to vary copy to suit the audience (also an aspect of targeting); personalized letters which read as though addressed to a public meeting; patronizing or being downright rude to the customer; the fact that prize draws do work; and the lack of imagination used in devising promotional offers.

In two respects he is wrong. Prize draws almost invariably work, no matter how rich the audience. And January is a very good month to sell anything, including books. But otherwise, I applaud everything he says.

NOTE: Even I can't remember who masterminded the liar Clinton's campaign, though to be paid to lie on behalf of someone who does it superbly without help speaks volumes. But I do remember this man's face. He was having it off with the woman who did the same job for Clinton's opponent. I think they got married. Maybe, instead of making love, they call each other shitty names all day long.

And who the hell was Clinton's opponent? I don't remember that either; but I do know who said that one day everyone would be famous for 15 minutes. It was Andy Warhol. He started out, would you believe, in advertising. Some would say he never left it. Maybe, boring as he was, he made more impact on our collective memory than many US presidents.

□ □ □

DATE: MARCH 1993

GOD IS IN THE DETAILS

You may have noticed I regularly monitor the work of the Ministry of Wasted Marketing Money and report on how they are fulfilling their remit. After all, your money as seller or buyer – and maybe both – is invested generously in their splendid initiatives.

The Spectator, which I have read for 18 years, has just invited me to become a subscriber with an offer so enticing I really must cancel my old subscription and accept. This generosity will cost them money needlessly, but I see it as an inadvertent long-service reward. How did it happen? They have a record of me in Somerset but not London and have failed in the difficult task of de-duplication.

This is understandable, unlike a silly letter from the European Direct Marketing Association, which you might

> I don't know what they do to other prospects or members… but if that's their idea of attention to detail they must irritate the living shit out of them.

think would have some clue about mailings, or even running an association. It begins 'Dear Sir or Madam'. To be fair, some time ago a reader suggested 'Drayton' could be male or female, but this is a special case. I sat for some time on the EDMA board, have spoken at several of their events, have written a column for years in their newsletter and have two books, one translated into six European languages, which are regularly sold by them to their members.

I don't know what EDMA do to other prospects or members (I am obviously a member) but if that's their idea of attention to detail they must irritate the living shit out of them. I simply had a queasy feeling about the future of Europe, which first surfaced years ago when I presented the prizes at their awards ceremony. It was a nightmare, because they made me do it in a sort of stuttering fashion. I conferred some prizes before the first course, others after the first course, more after the second course, yet more after the third and, believe it or not, a final batch (which few will have noticed) after dinner when most were roaring drunk.

I can't resist free offers. BT wrote to me last year saying I spent so much with them I could have a free mobile phone. If you read these maudlin meanderings you know I hate mobile phones, but greed swiftly resolved what could have been a taxing moral dilemma. My PA, the increasingly frantic Denise, arranged delivery of the infernal machine. I have never used it or even tried to understand how to; I have enough trouble anyhow avoiding people who want to contact me without making it easier for them. However, as a sign of BT's headlong pursuit of the best principles of customer service, they wrote thanking me for my order – nearly three months later.

As I have pointed out before in these columns, one of my clients at American Express in New York once calculated that there are over a hundred steps – 127, I think – to executing a direct mail campaign properly. Many people who should know better never get past steps one, two and three: get the name and address right; don't offend people; and mail out on time.

□ □ □

DATE: APRIL 1997

HOW ORDINARY PEOPLE LIVE

In recent months I have undergone two gruelling experiences: speaking solo for three days with simultaneous translation to audiences in both Madrid and Barcelona. But never mind my suffering: what about the audiences'? Spanish courtesy is legendary, but I was astonished how patiently they endured the endless hours. Not only did no one leave – they even applauded at the end.

Perhaps the applause expressed relief, but when they sent me nice letters afterwards I decided my mesmeric charm and oratory even survive being transmitted via another language. This ballooning complacency was punctured when I learnt the seminars were free to members of the Spanish Direct Marketing Association. Do people appreciate things more if they have to pay for

> **Most people in marketing lead lives so far removed from their customers' that they don't really know them.**

them than if they get them free? Either way, only the bliss provided by vast piles of bullion will persuade me to do it again.

Nevertheless, I often find such events educational – for me if not the audience. This time I learnt about some direct mail by an electricity company, aimed at poor people who can't pay their bills – folk who often don't even have bank accounts. A scheme based on their past bills was concocted. They could pay a monthly sum, which would not go up for a year. The next year it would be adjusted up or down as appropriate. No more nasty letters or phone calls, and their budgeting would be much easier. It was very simple to enrol in the scheme: people just had to sign.

A wonderful idea – but when a mailing was sent out the response was miserably low. Another mailing produced equally pathetic results. Then somebody decided to try some research. (I am often amazed how rarely people who run unsuccessful direct mail programmes bother to contact a few recipients and learn the answers to such strategic questions as 'Do you remember receiving the mailing?' not to mention 'Did you understand it?' and 'If not, why not?')

In this case the mailings had gone to the man of the family, but in such households it seems the woman usually handles the finances. These women were unlikely to open their husbands' mail – and even less likely to if it looked as though it might be a bill.

A new mailing was aimed at the women. Many people imagine men are attracted most by pictures of naked women and women by pictures of handsome men. However, pupil dilation tests suggest men look more at men, and women look more at women – but even more at babies. The new mailing looked like the announcement of a new baby, the infant in question being this new scheme. It was a howling (sorry) success.

This little tale illustrates two important truths. First, unless you fully understand your prospects you won't succeed. Second, most people in marketing lead lives so far removed from their customers' that they don't really know them. No wonder many if not most ads and mailings in Spain, the UK and just about anywhere else are poorly aimed (often at other marketing people) or incomprehensible, or both – like my seminars in Spain, for all I know.

□ □ □

DATE: MARCH 1996

LESSONS FROM SUCCESSFUL MAILINGS

Since most of you are spending more on direct mail than ever, you might like to know something about what works best. The place to find out is in *Million Dollar Mailings* (1992), a splendid book put together by the US publisher of *Who's Mailing What!* – not to be confused with the UK's *Who's Mailing What?* – which is, I believe, a copy of the original.

This book analyses 71 of the best US mailings ever – which the editors describe as 'Grand Controls', with priceless advice, much of it from their creators. Your 'control' mailing is the one that works best for you, so these mailings are those that have beaten everything they were tested against for the

> The word 'FREE' was plastered all over the outer envelopes... (disproving the silly theory that business people don't like to get something for nothing).

longest time in the world's largest, most competitive market. One, for the *Wall Street Journal*, has now been working with only minor changes for 23 years, pulling in about $1.3 billion.

Many of their characteristics may surprise you. Not one tried to conceal its intentions by masquerading as personal mail, 63 had messages on the envelope and 83 per cent had window envelopes. Most were inserted so the beginning of the letter is seen first. Almost every letter ignored the amateur's rule that you shouldn't exceed one page in length. The average length of letter to sell a consumer magazine was 3.3 pages; for business magazines, 2.1 pages. To sell a newsletter the average was 4 pages; for a home study course, 6 pages.

Free offers were the rule, whether to consumers or business people – and were even more common in the latter case. As you would expect, the word

'FREE' was plastered all over the outer envelopes, and was used in 71 per cent of business-to-business efforts (disproving the silly theory that business people don't like to get something for nothing). Eighty-three per cent asked people to 'send no money now'. Perhaps this is one reason why only 14 per cent, to my surprise, offered credit card facilities. I was even more surprised that so few offered the phone or fax ordering option that the editors didn't even bother to count them. They commented, 'For low-price products and services, the cost of in-bound telemarketing will eat you up.'

People often ask me if real stamps lift response. Nearly all these mailings use printed indicia, though people keep testing stamps. One mailer, from Book-of-the-Month Club, says they use stamps when the mailing is intended to look first class rather than very commercial. Apart from that, few mailings rely on the miracles of technology; only 25 per cent use elaborate personalization. Nor do they rely on famous agencies; only 10 per cent came from the multinationals, the remainder being by freelancers, in-house writers and 'boutiques'.

What use is a book of successful US mailings in the UK? More than you may think. Not only do the principles that apply in the USA work in the UK, so do many of the mailings – the *Wall Street Journal* effort, for one. Moreover, since people in the United States receive much more direct mail than those in the UK – six times more the last time I looked – US mailings must work harder to succeed. That's why I also strongly recommend *Who's Mailing What!* itself.

NOTE: You won't find *Who's Mailing What!* any more. Its founder has retired. But the publication carries on, renamed *Inside Direct Mail* and is still worth reading.

□ □ □

DATE: OCTOBER 1997

PEANUTS AND MONKEYS

I adore American lingo. They have a much livelier approach to our not always common language, as my American wife sometimes demonstrates during our more heated exchanges.

Maybe our culture is less able to innovate, but for whatever reason, I collect pithy lines like 'If you pay peanuts, you get monkeys' – which came to mind when considering, not for the first time, why direct marketing has a bad reputation.

Direct marketers hate being associated with 'junk'. But most door-to-door, direct mail and direct response advertising **is** junk. Ill conceived, carelessly executed, poorly targeted, it does the industry no credit. I don't think the practitioners alone are to blame, though. Clients who invest – or do not, as the whim takes them – are guilty.

> **C** lients... felt it... should either be 'free', like their advertising, or as part of the service.

First, they equate direct marketing with direct mail, which to them often signifies sales letters. Since they themselves write letters every day, they feel any fool can write a sales letter. Having written more than most – and just about everything else, from speeches to scripts to books – I can tell you that writing a good sales letter is no easier than writing an advertisement or commercial. Maybe harder. Few people can write persuasively to large numbers without losing that essential individual feeling.

A second reason is the way most clients are used to paying for advertising. Although changing now, traditionally it has been pretty painless because of the commission system. It almost feels as though they are getting the thinking and creative work for nothing. So when direct marketing started to attract their interest, most clients naturally felt it too should either be 'free', like their advertising, or as part of the service their agency provided, or as a low cost add-on, to be furnished in the same way as media analysis or sales literature.

This attitude was exacerbated by agencies' feelings that direct marketing was at best merely a 'line extension' or, at worst, a threat to their expertise, to be devalued.

A further problem is that many sales promotion houses claim to be expert at direct mail, which few are, and churn out mailings unencumbered by thought or knowledge. Even worse, quite a few are unencumbered by a letter to the recipient – although even the most mediocre direct marketer knows the letter is the most important part of a mailing pack.

If it is difficult to create direct marketing communications, it is even harder to execute them without making mistakes. This was brought home to me by a US client who discovered there are 127 steps to putting together a mailing programme – or to put it another way, 127 opportunities to get it wrong. A lot more complicated than dashing off a quick letter.

To give you an idea how much you ought to pay for direct mail, let me give you two figures I came across over the last few months: a leading advertising agency charges a major client £40,000 to create a new poster; and the US's top direct marketing agency charges $40,000 for a mailing pack.

In the UK few pay as much as one third of that sum for a mailing pack; however, looking at the price of the poster, I think it's quite cheap.

NOTE: Although written a few years ago, much of the above remains true.

□ □ □

DATE: NOVEMBER 1993

THE BASICS

The direct marketing industry sometimes reminds me of the sort of clichés journalists trot out about Third World countries, for example, 'I was astonished to see peasants toiling in the age-old immemorial fashion beneath the shadow of nuclear reactors.'

The direct marketer can do remarkable things. A publication can customize editorial and advertising to match the individual needs of millions of readers. Through the wonders of regression analysis you can review the performance of customers over time, then profile new prospects and by comparing their characteristics calculate their profit potential over a period of years. In this way you can determine how much you should invest to recruit and retain them.

> **S**adly to this day I am collecting ludicrously misdirected communications, like the one addressed to my secretary recently offering a cure for baldness.

Giant new printing machines exist whereby a sheet of paper enters at one end, and a complete catalogue, replete with rub-off patches, tear-off strips, reflecting surfaces and who knows what else emerges at the other. In a new Spanish TV initiative, viewers can 'interact' – to use a ghastly word – with programmes, being able, for instance, to join in and play a vacuous game show as it happens in the studio, or select discounts for products featured in the commercials.

Such marvels engage the lively imaginations of practitioners to an extraordinary degree. Most are obsessed with the future, while few concern themselves with the past, from which much can be learnt, or the present, when much is inadequate or even laughable. Too often the industry is attempting aerial acrobatics when at best it can barely crawl. Consider how stunningly inadequate most remain in the high strategy of addressing an envelope correctly.

Ten years ago at conferences I would show an envelope addressed to me that had on it 'personal', 'persönlich' and 'personel' – three different languages used in the hope that one would be relevant. Impersonalization in action. Sadly to this day I am collecting ludicrously misdirected communications, like the one addressed to my secretary recently offering a cure for baldness. Denise may have her shortcomings, though I have noticed few, but this could never be one of them.

By one of those fickle freaks of fate, some of the worst offenders are direct marketing 'professionals'. Many a quiet chuckle may be heard as *cognoscenti* exchange stories about the duplication of communications from the Direct Marketing Centre or the inadequacies of the UK Direct Marketing Association list.

A splendid instance occurred lately when Colvin Direct wrote to promise they would add punch to my direct mail and make it personal. They certainly knocked me out by the clever ploy of addressing me as a hermaphrodite: Mr/Ms D Bird. Understandable, perhaps, if they were writing to Drayton, conceivably a female name, but as I say, they wrote to me as **D** Bird. I am astonished that they did not have the wit to do the obvious: omit the Mr/Ms altogether and assume I would respond to D Bird.

Maybe all this is just another case of the tailor being the worst-dressed man in the room, but I find it depressing that alleged experts can't get the **very** basic things right.

□ □ □

DATE: NOVEMBER 1992

THE LINE STOPS HERE

Have you ever wondered why so much direct mail looks as though it's been tossed off by three monkeys with a typewriter sitting in an attic? Or why the tone of much sales promotion brings the *Sunday Sport* inexorably to mind?

The blame must lie to some degree at the door of the bean-counter at Unilever (or was it Procter & Gamble?) who innocently drew the infamous line on his budget sheet, above which advertising chaps float trailing clouds of ineffable glory, and below which lurk the oily rags employed in sales promotion and direct marketing.

I will not dwell on the psychic wounds inflicted upon **me** by this concept, but rather on the damage it does to many marketing efforts. The mere phrase 'below-the-line' implies that all

> US research by Starch a while ago revealed that customers in California were exposed to 623 advertising impressions daily, of which they only remembered 9 favourably 24 hours later.

activities under such a category, even if they are necessary, certainly do not require much intellectual fire-power. They should be accomplished with as little expenditure and effort as possible so we can all get back to the more important matter of the music track on our new TV commercial.

If you find this example far-fetched, let me tell you that in a meeting not long ago, that is precisely what happened: we spent 57 minutes discussing the music track for my client's new commercial and just three minutes discussing the direct marketing which produces most of their business.

Mind you, I have some sympathy with this sort of thing, bearing in mind that the commercial in question cost about as much as a Spike Lee movie. However, direct marketing in particular uses highly intrusive media like direct mail and the telephone. To send out badly aimed stuff that does not reflect your brand values through these media is a very expensive mistake.

US research by Starch a while ago revealed that customers in California were exposed to 623 advertising impressions daily, of which they only remembered 9 favourably 24 hours later. Three actually left a bad impression. Conversely, my agency discovered that one mailing to frequent fliers was recalled by 74 per cent after four months. We repeated the research for a cosmetics mailing: the figure was 70 per cent after three months – so the first finding was not an aberration.

Cato the Elder used to end all his speeches with '*Delenda est Carthago*' (Carthage must be destroyed) until eventually all the other Romans agreed with him and did destroy Carthage.

Now, ensuring your direct marketing receives the same level of attention as your advertising is not as critical as the Third Punic War. Nevertheless, I think it important enough to return to from time to time in the months that lie ahead, in the hope that eventually standards will rise appropriately.

NOTE: I include this piece partly for sentimental reasons, as it was the first I wrote for *Marketing*, but partly because eight and a half years later it is still relevant.

Change in this world is much slower than we think. Most direct mail is still garbage, but the good stuff still makes a very strong impression. A letter my agency sent to older customers for a bank a few months ago was recalled by 97 per cent a month later.

The client who spent so much time on the music track was the top advertising man at American Express in New York. Being a gentleman, he actually apologized to me for wasting my time.

□ □ □

DATE: MAY 1991

THE LINGERING DEATH OF MASS MARKETING

Pundits divide marketing into three eras: the age of mass marketing – speaking to **everyone**; the age of segmentation – speaking to **some people**; and now, the age when people are trying to speak to **individuals**, which is best achieved by using direct marketing.

I have been as guilty as anybody of over-simplifying in that way, so I found the following interesting: 'Every age, they say, has its special bit of nonsense. The 18th century had its noble savage, and the 19th its automatic progress. **Now** we have this modern nonsense about the mass man.' Novelist Joyce Carey wrote that some 40 years ago. I found it in the *Advertising Age* issue of 20 June 1955, quoted in an article written by Nicholas Samstag of *Time* magazine.

> In 1955, the Chevrolet Sedan 210 line offered so many options that every man, woman and child in Oshkosh, Wisconsin (population 41,084) could buy a four-door sedan, and no two of them would be exactly alike.

He also revealed a number of other interesting facts about those far-off days. In 1955, the Chevrolet Sedan 210 line offered so many options that every man, woman and child in Oshkosh, Wisconsin (population 41,084) could buy a four-door sedan, and no two of them would be exactly alike. He added that Chevrolet had several other lines.

He had some other interesting findings. In the United States at that time 78 per cent of discretionary income was in the hands of 10 per cent of the families. So the Pareto Principle – that a very small percentage of people in any market spend most of the money – operated then, as it always has done.

Now, you might imagine that the readers of *Advertising Age*, fired by these thoughts, would in 1955 immediately have made an earnest endeavour to move into targeted marketing, that they would have concentrated on the wealthy few, offering them individually tailored products based upon their personal needs. Of course, nothing of the sort happened, except to some extent at *Time* magazine, where they seem to have done rather well since then.

Most marketers have continued to operate along exactly the same lines as they did then, as though the mass market is the only thing that matters. In this country, for instance, they operate under the delusion that it makes sense to spend £20 million in mass media, selling shares in the public utilities, when much the same results could be achieved through the free medium of the regular bill.

However, all is not lost. If Peter Drucker is correct in thinking that it takes 40 years for a new development to come to full fruition in our society, then we shall witness – in about five years – the triumph of the age of individualized, intelligent, cost-effective marketing. None too soon – but too late for some.

NOTE: Of course, I was far too optimistic. I wrote this in May 1991. There is now, in November 1999, a great deal of hot air about 'one-to-one' marketing, but very little done. Names and addresses continue to be erroneous; people who have not shopped in a store for a year still get clichéd letters that begin with the turgid formula, 'As a valued customer'.

Only the other day one marketer commented that she was often written to by firms who assume she is a man. And of course marketers continue to shy away from the perils of having the results of their efforts measured. No wonder, when you see some of the antics they get up to.

□ □ □

DATE: MAY 1991

WHY DIRECT MARKETING MAKES SUCH SENSE

When last year the jamborees of the US Association of National Advertisers and the US Direct Marketing Association took place, the former attracted about 500 — and was so dull even *Advertising Age* noticed. The latter pulled in about 10,000.

These numbers reflect a trend that has been going on for years, and has been noted, but not acted on sufficiently by many, especially in advertising agencies. Whilst prattling happily about the end of the recession they fail to note that the traditional light at the end of the tunnel is indeed that of an oncoming train — which will squash many of them if they're not careful.

> **Y**our database reveals which people are most profitable… British Airways sell over 26 million flights a year but concentrate on 750,000 customers.

I shall view the carnage with equanimity, having spent thankless years preaching the direct marketing gospel to my advertising brethren at Ogilvy & Mather. They paid lip-service, but little more, as one story illustrates. In the mid-80s we invited the creative director of O & M to speak to our direct people. Nearly all my staff came to hear what he had to say, which was trivial but delivered quite well. David Ogilvy asked me, 'Is there going to be a return match?' I said, 'I doubt it,' as I had seen few signs of intelligent curiosity at the agency. However, eventually one took place. Of their 300 staff, five turned up.

Little has changed. A while ago an ex-Ogilvy office MD told me he was setting something up 'above the line', adding half-guiltily, 'not that the phrase means anything any more'. Although this man is no fool, I'd bet all the tea in China to a bent tin watch that he has never seriously studied anything other than advertising. Such curious myopia explains why most 'through-the-line' agencies, being founded by advertising people, do so poorly – and even the successful ones don't do direct work well.

I have tried to give up my evangelistic practices, but maybe it's worth restating why direct marketing has grown and will grow, whatever fancy label people slap on it – relationship marketing, loyalty marketing, one-to-one marketing and so on.

First, you know rather than guess what your investment returns. I remain astonished that anyone other than a half-wit thinks it wise to spend money without knowing the results except in terms of awareness and attitude shift, when a keyed response device tells you exactly what pays and what doesn't. You will learn, for instance, that your customer is between three and eight times more responsive than a similar non-customer, and that a promotional responder is twice as likely to buy. Second, your database reveals which people are most profitable, so you can build a stronger bond with them rather than squander money indiscriminately. Thus, British Airways sell over 26 million flights a year but concentrate on 750,000 customers. Third, since the database shows you what characterizes your current customers you can learn how to locate new ones, because the customer you want is like the customer you've got.

These inescapable realities are why lip-service is not enough: real understanding is required if you wish to survive the next 10 years as competition sharpens and the focus moves more and more to accountability.

□ □ □

DATE: FEBRUARY 1996

JUNK JOURNALISM

My daughter tells me there is a primitive tribe amongst whom it is traditional to greet people by seizing them warmly but firmly by one hand whilst grasping their testicles vigorously with the other.

This is, of course, not unlike the standard ritual in British journalism, which I should have remembered when an insipid little man called Keeling from the *Evening Standard* interviewed me a while ago for the purpose of an article entitled, oh-so-wittily, 'Rogue Mail'.

Now I can't really complain that the article misrepresented me, because it gave many a chortle to my friends and colleagues, furnished my wife with an excuse to redecorate my office and produced five enquiries from prospective clients. Also, I have been known to misrepresent one or two people myself in these pages.

> The paper consumed by direct mail is minuscule compared to that gobbled up by popular newspapers.

What I do wonder is where this louse on the locks of literature gets the gall to talk about junk mail in a magazine containing 96 pages of trivia including pieces on such riveting subjects as people with interesting swimming pools, with the usual dollop of eminently forgettable information in the accompanying newspaper.

The underlying theme of his piece was that people in our business are the lowest of the low – a case bolstered rather unfortunately by one of the other interviewees, who clearly felt his social status would be raised if he were to get a job in an abattoir.

Sadly, direct marketers are not on a par with Mother Teresa, Nobel Prize winners or nurses, but rather bracketed with such lowly groups as minor members of the royal family, politicians and, most wholeheartedly reviled of all, journalists like Mr Keeling.

I quite went off people like him in 1970 when one newspaper libelled my company, leaving me helpless despite the fact that counsel told me I had an impeccable case. I simply wasn't rich enough to sit it out through legal proceedings.

The skills required to do his job were well defined by an infinitely better journalist, Nicholas Tomalin, who said it only required 'rat-like cunning, a plausible manner, and a little literary ability'. I have more sympathy with the honest muckraking of the *Sun* or even the *Sunday Sport* than with the pretensions of the quasi-quality press.

At least Keeling spared us the chopping-down-the-forests routine – irrelevant on two counts, since the paper used for print comes from forests which are being replenished faster than they are used up, and the paper consumed by direct mail is minuscule compared to that gobbled up by popular newspapers.

I think his editor should commission him to examine the reasons why the national press has for some time had a declining circulation, whilst year after year surveys indicate that direct mail in this country wins more acceptance from both business and public.

Have a nice day, Mr Keeling.

NOTE: Six years later, the print and broadcast media are still churning out the same sort of stuff, direct mail continues to thrive and I am honing a rat-like cunning. Mr Keeling, I hope, is unemployed.

□ □ □

DATE: AUGUST 1993

Lessons from Great Minds and Nitwits

Introduction

You can learn a lot about what to do by studying how the best people go about things. But I sometimes wonder whether you don't learn more by watching how things go wrong. That way you know what to avoid.

In this selection you will find examples of both wisdom and folly. I hope you find it instructive.

AN OVERCROWDED MARKET

I don't know how many of you study the stock market, but the only thing I know is you must buy low and sell high. The problem of course is that nobody ever seems to know either when a rising market has yet to peak or a falling market has hit bottom.

The people who got it most spectacularly right were the Rothschilds. The legend is that in 1815 they bought shares amazingly cheaply on the London Stock Exchange just before the news of Wellington's victory at Waterloo became generally known. Allegedly they knew about it before anyone else through the advanced technology of a carrier pigeon – though I have heard that this is all just a good story. Whether that is so or not, I remembered it when reflecting on the monstrous regiment of companies who are now selling insurance direct, inspired in many cases by the triumphs of Mr Wood, late of Direct Line.

> **T**his market (insurance) is a perfect example of the classic business case study where lots of people do some research... and then separately conclude they should go into the same business.

At a loss what to do one morning, I analysed all the display advertising in a recent issue of the *Daily Mail*. Nearly 20 per cent of it was selling insurance directly. This leads me to conclude that there will be tears before bedtime for many of these firms. Indeed, since drafting this I see one has dropped out of the field. This market is a perfect example of the classic business case study where lots of people do some research (that is, see a host of red Direct Line phones on TV, followed by announcements of Mr Wood's astonishing income) and then separately conclude they should go into the same business.

One reason why I am rather pessimistic is that it is not only the same business, but they're all offering the same proposition: we'll save you money. No ludicrous device has been ignored in an effort to get the story over. My favourite is the admiral taking his sabre to slash rates, though the Churchill bulldog has a certain kitsch charm.

I must confess an interest here. I was approached by a motoring organization some months ago that didn't know what to do about their insurance offering. Their prices weren't very keen, and price was what was selling. I pointed out, it seemed to me reasonably, that whilst most people are interested in price, and nobody likes paying for insurance, there are always some who think differently and might be motivated by other things – like better service.

They seemed, with some difficulty, to grasp this concept, which is not really all that intellectually demanding, but they were never able to summon up sufficient courage to run the advertising I proposed. Vainly I reasoned with them. It would have cost just £2,000–£3,000 to test the concepts, and goodness knows how much money they could have made if they succeeded. A lost opportunity.

I am encouraged to see that Mr Wood, who is about £50 million cleverer than me, seems to think the price angle has been done to death too. As far as I can make out his new venture will appeal to the segment of the market that has been neglected – 'high-risk' drivers, or drunken lunatics, as we call them in Somerset.

NOTE: Peter Wood persuaded the Bank of Scotland to back him in setting up Direct Line, a firm selling motor insurance directly. Their symbol was a red telephone on wheels. He made a fortune as a result, and was widely copied, not just in Britain, but all over the world.

The timorous motoring organization I mention was the RAC.

□ □ □

DATE: MARCH 1995

EDUCATION: COULD IT BE THE DEATH OF MARKETING?

Nobody is more devoted to education than I am. I spend far too much time teaching for rather less money than I make at my normal trade. But education, if it is to be good, has to have some relationship, however loose, to real life. From what I have learnt recently, this is far from the case with some of the teaching conducted by that otherwise blameless body, The Chartered Institute of Marketing.

A colleague has been studying with them, and some of the things he has been told are so ludicrous they make me fear for the future of marketing, besides explaining why much is so ill conducted. Not long ago, for instance, he was told by one clown that direct marketing falls under sales promotion; whilst when discussing a project to sell 432,000 leotards a year at £10 a throw, the same demented loon blithely suggested – without any attempt at calculation – that £1 million would be a sensible advertising budget. Since the imaginary firm's entire turnover was only about four times as much, not unnaturally my associate remonstrated with her.

> The same demented loon blithely suggested – without any attempt at calculation – that £1 million would be a sensible advertising budget.

This piece of eminent good sense produced a paroxysm of wrath from the pulpit. My boy was told to belt up and see the lady in question later. I have to admit he didn't, the disobedient dog, perhaps because his character lacks the necessary streak of masochism. I'm not even sure about that, though, since it seems very like self-torture to go and listen to people in your own time, paying your own good money, to be told such utter tosh.

To give you some idea of how pathetic standards are, I now enter in evidence a paragraph from a typical handout. 'Strategies – how to get there – follow on from objectives. In this case we are dealing with achieving/fulfilling plans that may be long-term strategic plans, but strategies do not relate necessarily to the longer term, although logically, as they derive from objectives, strategies should be consistent with the strategic approach.'

What the deuce does that mean? I can't get my head round it at all. Can you? In fact, I'll be very happy to send a bottle of decent wine to anyone able to make sense of it. I will be even happier if somebody at the CIM takes a long cold hard look at their teachers and their teaching. Based on what I have seen, a faculty of unemployed bus conductors could hardly do worse. Some of the current bunch will, if unchecked, fatally poison the fragile roots of tomorrow's marketing.

As you will recall, acidulous old George Bernard Shaw observed, 'He who can, does. He who cannot, teaches.' I have to be honest and say that this has sometimes made me question my own pedagogical forays; but after spending a little time looking into what the CIM is doing I feel quite uplifted to realize that, comparatively, I may be one of the few tottering bastions of sense in a deranged world.

□ □ □

DATE: DECEMBER 1996

60

IN WHICH WE PONDER THE MYSTERIES OF EMPLOYMENT

A friend just wrote suggesting these pages are 'preoccupied with half-wits blowing lots of other people's money, getting fired and turning up to do it all over again somewhere else. I've now concluded, with some sadness, that marketing has ousted architecture from the bottom of the professional competence table'.

This is unfair to our newshounds, who after all can only report the facts. It also ignores the claims of social workers, economists and teachers. Surely we can't be as culpable as many of them? At least we don't destroy families, cripple entire national economies, or render whole generations illiterate, innumerate and morally derelict.

> **A** friend in Sydney once rang me because his firm was about to hire, unvetted, an English direct marketer. 'Is he any good?' he asked. 'A fine man for a fast tax loss,' I replied.

Indeed, we even make up some of these disasters by taking nigh-unemployable graduates off the streets to write impenetrable, jargon-clotted research documents and marketing plans, which luckily for them no one reads.

Some professions' sins find them out more surely than others'. Who remembers the names of the horde of economists who wrote to Mrs Thatcher saying she was wrong in what she was doing with the economy? Did any lose their jobs as a result? How many 'caring workers' are clapped in jail for the misery they inflict on families? But each disgusting building that architects design testifies, until it falls down or is demolished, to their bad taste and incompetence, just as for us each sight of the sales graph does much the same.

It takes longer, though, for Sir James Stirling to design a masterpiece than it does to reposition a soft drink; and longer still for anyone to notice the roof leaks, by which time another dumb committee has coughed up for something else on the other side of the world. With us, the process is quicker; in under two years the average marketing director has been hired, had a go, and either been found out, or done well and moved ahead. But why do the duds get good jobs in the first place?

Oddly enough, people often take less care hiring senior marketers than secretaries, which is maybe why secretaries keep their jobs longer. The criterion is, nine times out of ten: has the person done this sort of job before, not: how good is this person? One obvious question is rarely asked: if the person's that good, why is he or she looking for a job? They often don't even talk to previous employers. A friend in Sydney once rang me because his firm was about to hire, unvetted, an English direct marketer. 'Is he any good?' he asked. 'A fine man for a fast tax loss,' I replied, since he had just helped lose his previous firm so much money so quickly they went broke.

Many people are kicked out because their firms lack patience. How can the effects of years of folly be overcome in 18 months? Other, worthier candidates for the chop thrive unpunished. Remember Pepsi squandering $300 million or was it $500 million on 'relaunching' their product in new cans, much of it wasted on silly gimmicks like painting Concorde blue for a day? When sales slumped was the big boss fired? No. Yet he's presided over years of decline. Was the person responsible fired? No – promoted. Funny old business, this.

NOTE: I see I had forgotten when I wrote the introduction to this book that the rewards for failure at Pepsi Cola are also promotion, which shows how similar they really are to their great rival, Coke.

☐ ☐ ☐

DATE: MARCH 1997

IT'S HIDEOUS, BUT IS IT ART?

My second wife Anna yearned to paint, to which end she took a part-time course for a year before going to Maidstone Art College full time. She found it very disappointing, poor darling, because she wanted to draw and paint well. At Maidstone they scorned such trivia, concentrating more on teaching their charges to express themselves.

To be fair, Anna used to express herself amazingly well, if my memory of our spectacular rows is any guide; but that wasn't quite what her teachers had in mind. They were keener on the sort of self-expression displayed by Maidstone graduate Tracey Emin, recently described as 'one of Britain's foremost young artists' in *The Big Issue*.

> **F**rom then on it is but a modest step to saying you can take anything – Gilbert and George's turds, for instance – and say it's a work of art.

Her mind uncluttered by curiosity about anything except herself, Tracey's impressive marketing skills far exceed her artistic talents. She even has her own museum near Waterloo where she proves beyond doubt that she didn't waste her time learning to draw, concentrating rather on being 'fiercely creative'. Her dreary self-absorption makes her the only possible subject of all her work, and her latest masterpiece, *Everyone I've Ever Slept With 1963–1995*, is revealingly vast. She bullshits fluently about her 'painful, joyous and unfalteringly direct' art in that phoney, streetwise way best calculated to beguile idiot critics and Turner Prize judges. Apparently, her inspiration wells up from no ordinary artistic source, but from an abortion, an experience after which, she eloquently notes, 'You can't make fucking paintings, not honestly... I stopped making art 'cos I was so fucking naff at it.' If her current *œuvre* is any guide little has changed.

Who started all this nonsense? Take a bow, Marcel Duchamp, Belgian surrealist prankster. One day after a drunken lunch he submitted a urinal to an art exhibition in Philadelphia as a joke, signing it R Mutt, 1917. Things in Philadelphia being the way they are, it was accepted. From then on it is but a modest step to saying you can take anything – Gilbert and George's turds, for instance – and say it's a work of art.

We've come a long way from William Hogarth's approach, yet I fear the seminal works of Ms Emin, amusing though they are, may not last the course as well as his. This year is the tercentenary of his birth, and it's ironic that *The Big Issue* hasn't noticed it, since if any painter's work reflects street life, his does. It's more than ironic –it's disgraceful – that whilst loudmouth Tracey has her museum, no major exhibition of Hogarth, one of this country's greatest painters, is planned as far as I know.

It is interesting to reflect how the oddities of today's education affect the work of those of us who communicate to sell. We already have a situation where many copywriters, weaned on a restricted diet of 30-second TV commercials, are exhausted by the effort of writing more than 90 words, baffled by the mysteries of the apostrophe and can often only determine with difficulty the infinitely subtle differences between singular and plural.

And it's years since I met a young art director who could draw well. Come back, Anna: all is forgiven.

NOTE: Only the other day, reading about the Turner Prize, I saw that Tracey Emin continues to be regarded as one of Britain's foremost young artists, though I have no idea how many more people she has generously favoured with her charms lately. God knows what Turner would have thought. Anna has not come back, which is just as well, really.

□ □ □

DATE: APRIL 1997

64

LESSONS FROM AMERICAN MAIL ORDER ROGUES

In the 60s my education was significantly advanced by meeting a number of US mail order operators, some none too scrupulous. They realized there were fortunes to be made in Europe, though very few succeeded because there were quite a few ingenious rogues here already.

The leading US mail order speciality operator went into partnership with a clever Belgian who outwitted him at every turn. One day the mail order operator came to visit the Belgian in his rather neat little penthouse with the modest address, 'The Sun Tower, Monte Carlo'. His host showed him the view over the harbour and asked if he liked it. 'I've got to. I paid for it,' the operator replied.

> **S**lumberslim... would lose you pounds of ugly flab 'through the miracle of auto-oxidation'. When I asked the genius responsible what that was, he said, 'Sweating, kid. Sweating.'

Some of the US scams were hilarious. Slumberslim, for instance, would lose you pounds of ugly flab 'through the miracle of auto-oxidation'. When I asked the genius responsible what that was, he said, 'Sweating, kid. Sweating.' It was legal because you could make outrageous claims about a book and get away with it, as they are only the author's opinions. (You still can.) The guarantee was brilliant: if you're not happy, just tear the cover off the book, send it back and you'll get your money back. (You didn't.) This man eventually found his natural home selling pornography in Denmark.

My favourite scamp was Monroe. He was a superb copywriter who would have done well anywhere. Unfortunately he suffered from a crippling disability: he simply couldn't bring himself to tell the truth if it was at all possible to lie. One ad he ran sold fast-growing trees that did exactly that – grew extremely fast. That wasn't enough for him. He showed a man standing in front of a conifer about 10 times higher than him. The headline was, 'Just plant – and stand back!' Monroe made loads of money but never kept it. It all went to his lawyer to keep him out of jail.

I wonder how much we'll end up paying for the UK Government's dishonesty. I only ask because of something I commented on last year: the right of politicians to tell whoppers in election advertising – legally. I quoted lies about hospital waiting lists (now longer than ever) and school class sizes (now larger than ever). If this Government had to withstand the scrutiny poor old Monroe was subjected to, they'd all be in jail double-quick.

I saw recently that the Minister of Consumer Affairs, somebody called Griffiths, wants to stop holiday firms quoting misleading prices. Scandalous. But how does it compare with finding out my children are being badly taught or my old Gran will pop her clogs before she reaches hospital? When will Mr Griffiths stroll boldly into Number 10 to nick Mr Blair?

What disgusts me is the hypocrisy. Look at all the flannel they unloaded about encouraging saving. The reality is Mr Robinson's new ISA rip-off. As we know, he has salted away mountains of money offshore. Legal or not, I wonder how many people feel – as I do – that if he were as poor as the rest of us, he'd never get away with it. Putting him in charge of how our money should be invested is like appointing the head of the Medellin Cartel as a drug 'tsar'.

I suspect what the UK needs is an opposition party.

NOTE: Since I wrote this, everything has got worse. People with vested interests are giving more money than ever to the Labour Party. More people are waiting for operations. More children are being crowded into school classes. ISAs are a flop because no one understands them – and they're a worse deal than the things they replaced. And there is still no effective opposition party.

□   □   □

DATE: DECEMBER 1997

MORE THOUGHTS ABOUT PLANNING

I suppose one of the principal objectives of a columnist should be to provoke reaction – the more vehement the better. This can always be achieved by disputing current wisdom, which I did a few weeks ago by suggesting that importing planning from the advertising world was a silly idea for direct marketing agencies.

My iconoclasm earned me two out-raged letters to *Marketing* the very next week, plus a basilisk glare from the Head of Planning at O & M Direct the very next day.

All concerned were aghast, I suppose, that if such a view became popular, it might lead to a wave of unemployment amongst planners. So I

> **C**opying what advertising agencies are doing, no matter what specious intellectual allure may be on offer, is pretty dumb.

should make one point clear: it is neither planning nor planners I object to – the first is essential, the second tend to be intelligent – it is planning as a separate function or department.

In the letters three arguments emerged. The first can be quickly des-patched: one correspondent inferred, with no evidence, that I was only interested in response and not the impact of the marketer. Those who know me will realize this is balderdash as well as being irrelevant.

A second argument, equally ludicrous, was that surely creatives couldn't be expected to understand consumers. I would respond that it is precisely this ability that largely distinguishes good creative people from bad.

The third argument was that advertising would go downhill without planning. To realize what tripe this is, simply refer to the 60s, when Doyle Dane Bernbach, Collett Dickinson & Pearce, and others were creating advertising distinctly better than most of the stuff churned out today. One apposite example is John Webster of BMP, one of the cradles of planning. He was producing superb work before the days of planning, as were Charles Saatchi, Alan Parker, Tony Brignull and others.

Current wisdom applauds planning: indeed, agencies like Chiat Day and Wieden & Kennedy in the US have imported British planners to institute it. But is what is right for advertising right for direct marketing? Copying what advertising agencies are doing, no matter what specious intellectual allure may be on offer, is pretty dumb: as a group they are not doing as well as their direct marketing cousins.

Planning was introduced during the fat years of the early 70s, when budgets were growing and laxly supervised. But today most clients are cutting costs and reducing layers and functions. Generally agencies are wise to mirror their clients; why go the other way?

In short, I am all in favour of planning, but have grave doubts about having a separate department. Many clients find direct marketing agencies appeal because they have a simple approach to business without unnecessary frills – or departments. This attraction is going to increase rather than diminish as the present slump endures.

Oh, and by the way, at a recent meeting of the Database Marketing Group it became abundantly clear that direct marketers are not sure what planning is anyhow. Some saw it as preparing a mailing; others viewed it as making a marketing plan. How can you successfully institute something most people cannot define?

□　□　□

DATE: NOVEMBER 1992

MORE WAFFLE, LESS SENSE

A few years ago signs started popping up proclaiming the 'mission' of the agricultural college next door to my country home, a fine institution that had flourished for decades without such flim-flam. They read 'Quality Our Priority'. I don't know how they arrived at this – maybe to distinguish themselves from colleges who believe quality doesn't matter at all – but it was a good excuse for an article.

Shortly afterwards the signs disappeared. I felt mildly pleased, even foolishly thinking perhaps someone had read my piece. They must have spent almost as much removing the signs as erecting them. Such folly is one reason why, no matter how much money is squandered, education will not improve until stupid 'managers' are replaced by intelligent teachers who arrange their own affairs, as they did when people (including aspirant teachers) left school able to read, write and count. God alone knows when this or any government will learn this.

> **An incredible amount of time and energy is wasted on this sort of waffle by semi-literate, underemployed posers who should be given proper jobs requiring measurable results.**

Alas, I learnt my pleasure was unjustified when walking my dog through the college's pleasant grounds recently. The signs had only vanished because they have a new mission statement that couldn't conceivably fit on anything smaller than a 48-sheet poster.

Imagine the agonizing, scratching of heads and interminable committee meetings about commas and adjectives it took to produce something as ill written as this:

> Welcome to Cannington College. The mission at Cannington College is: to provide quality assured education and training, for people and businesses

involved with plants, animals, or environmentally sensitive land use. Everyone of 16 years or over is welcome at Cannington College, irrespective of background. A belief in equal opportunities underpins the whole philosophy of the college, as does a concern for the environment and for health and safety. Our hallmark is a friendly approach and a concern for the individual, combining a sense of fun with an innovative approach to quality assured education and training.

'Quality Our Priority' was hardly original, but it was at least short and clear. Saying you welcome anybody irrespective of background is at the very least open to misinterpretation and even abuse. What, for instance, if a coke-snorting alcoholic with no discernible signs of literacy applies for entry?

An incredible amount of time and energy is wasted on this sort of waffle by semi-literate, underemployed posers who should be given proper jobs requiring measurable results. It is a happy playground for lazy minds.

The beautiful priory which houses part of the college I refer to was built around the time when one of the few successful committees in history was engaged in producing perhaps the most beautiful book in English – the Authorized Version of the Bible. I say 'perhaps' because the Book of Common Prayer is maybe even more moving. It had its origins rather earlier, in the reign of Henry VIII.

Here's a sign from a hotel bedroom I stay in opposite one of Henry's haunts, Hampton Court. 'We endeavour at all times to operate our business in an environmentally aware manner without, of course, detracting from either our high standards of service and facilities or your personal comfort. We cannot, however, achieve our goal without your co-operation, and below are a few ways in which you can assist us if you so wish.'

That, believe it or not, introduces a plea to reuse your bath-towels. I sometimes fear we will all end up drowned in this creeping swamp of literary garbage – a point I have made several times before, but will not stop making while I write these columns.

☐ ☐ ☐

DATE: OCTOBER 1998

THE JOYS OF FOREIGN TRAVEL

In the office of the boss of Eurostar hangs a sign: 'Rule 1: The customer is always wrong. Rule 2: When in doubt, refer to Rule 1.' Actually, I made that up, but as far as I can see it's how they think.

A while ago my daughter, her baby and I had a little jaunt to France. On the way back difficult train connections meant I had to ring Eurostar in Paris to change our pre-booked train. No problem, they said, as long as I turned up a little in advance. Anyhow, the day deteriorated sharply and our train to Paris to link up with Eurostar was an hour late. Very thoughtfully, though, SNCF handed out envelopes to all of us to get a compensatory rebate, an idea our rail firms should copy. We got to the Gare du Nord in plenty of time for the train – but not to change the tickets, said the booking-office dragon.

> Eventually, not only did they replace the fittings on each bag, but also gave us a 50 per cent refund on the price of our order – which we used to buy more, better-made bags.

I explained the problem, and her magnificently moustachioed 'chef' appeared. He said I must pay for my daughter and myself – £200 – though he magnanimously let the baby on free. I protested. It wasn't my fault I was late but SNCF's – and showed my rebate envelope as proof. He was unmoved and suggested I write and complain.

I suspect he was smiling inwardly with glee because he knew the complaints department's mission statement – Rule 1: Reject all complaints. Rule 2: Refer to the boss's rules. However, they do have a profound sense of the ridiculous. They sent me two free tickets to the first-class lounge. When someone's talking about £200 down the drain the offer of a couple of cups of free coffee is as close to an insult as you could manage, besides ensuring the aggrieved party tells everyone he or she knows what arrogant tossers you are.

Compare their performance with that of Compass International, a relatively small firm. They did all they could to solve a minor problem. I had decided in a moment of madness to have 50 bags emblazoned with our pretty little logo. They had to be big and strong enough to carry laptop computers plus the usual loads of business bumph. When we got them we were very pleased, but the clips attaching the shoulder straps to the bags were not strong enough to bear a really heavy load, and tended to come apart. They tried repeatedly to solve the problem. Eventually, not only did they replace the fittings on each bag, but also gave us a 50 per cent refund on the price of our order – which we used to buy more, better-made bags.

They probably made more profit. They improved their product. They made an old man very happy. And they ensured that the next time I want a load of bags or I meet anybody else that does, I'll mention their name. On the other hand, the next time I want a load of old bollocks, I shall turn with quiet confidence to the complaints department at Eurostar.

□ □ □

DATE: MAY 1998

THE WISDOM OF LEO

A while ago I was flattered to be asked to contribute to a book about the future of direct marketing called *Beyond 2000*. It's been written by 27 US pundits plus a token foreigner – me. The idea came from Jerry Reitman of Leo Burnett.

Our elephantine tome will have to be very good to better a little booklet called *100 Leo's*, containing quotes from Leo Burnett, which I picked up at the launch press conference in Toronto. They missed out my favourite – 'If you absolutely insist on being different just for the sake of being different, you can always come down to breakfast with a sock in your mouth' – a wonderful indictment of those who think being strange or odd is the same as being creative. But here are some gems:

> **If you absolutely insist on being different just for the sake of being different, you can always come down to breakfast with a sock in your mouth.**

- One of the greatest dangers of advertising is not that of misleading people, but that of boring them to death.
- Good writing is rapidly becoming a lost art in advertising.
- Keep it simple. Let's do the obvious thing – the common thing – but let's do it uncommonly well.
- What helps people, helps business.
- If people could tell you in advance what they want, there would never have been a wheel, a lever, much less an automobile, an airplane or a TV set.
- We want consumers to say, 'That's a hell of a product,' instead of, 'That's a hell of an ad.'
- I listen to everybody and take notes. Particularly salesmen. They get close to people.
- Plan the sale when you plan the ad.
- The sole purpose of business is service. The sole purpose of advertising is

explaining the service which business renders.

- No one makes mistakes on purpose. Knowing this should allow us to concentrate on correcting the mistake rather than making life miserable for the mistake maker. If he is the right sort, nothing you can say or do to him will make him feel any worse than he does already.
- To swear off making mistakes is very easy. All you have to do is swear off having ideas.
- In this agency business we are people talking to people, and that's what we should keep running through our fingers.
- A really good creative person is more interested in earnestness than in glibness and takes more satisfaction out of converting people than in 'wowing' them.
- You have to make a friend before you can effectively make him a proposition.
- Any fool can write a bad ad, but it takes a real genius to keep his hands off a good one.
- The secret of all effective originality in advertising is not the creation of new and tricky words and pictures, but one of putting familiar words and pictures into new relationships.
- Fun without sell gets nowhere; but sell without fun tends to become obnoxious.
- Steep yourself in your subject, work like hell, and love, honour and obey your hunches.

Leo Burnett is now a great agency again, but they went through some rough years when they forgot about Leo. Others could learn from that. During the years I worked for Ogilvy & Mather, a surprising number of their people were dismissive of their founder and his thinking, but, as he once said to me, 'I made their bed. They lie on it.'

NOTE: Reading through this compendium, I see I mention David Ogilvy more than anyone else. No surprise. He had more influence on more people in advertising than anyone else this century. And advertising is the part of marketing that interests most people.

□ □ □

WHERE DOES TALENT COME FROM?

Remarkable people see things more clearly than us second-raters. Nine years ago David Ogilvy made a speech on recruitment to the panjandrums of his group, of whom I was then one. A friend had asked how his daughter might get into advertising. David suggested trying O & M – 'quite a good agency', he said mock-modestly. Months later he asked what had happened. It seems she never even got an interview because she didn't have an MBA.

To the distinctly muted hilarity of those present, who probably introduced it, David said this rule meant that nowadays he wouldn't get a job with his own firm; and what's more, because our clients paid newly qualified MBAs twice as much as we did, we would get the dross. He prescribed a typically trenchant and paradoxical course: 'Hire people your clients would never dream of hiring.' Though to be honest, since MBAs are taught how to run things before they know how they work, I strongly suspect wise firms should never hire them under any circumstances.

> Since MBAs are taught how to run things before they know how they work, I strongly suspect wise firms should never hire them under any circumstances.

Finding people and helping them do well is the hardest, yet I think most important job in business. You never really know where they're going to pop up, so you must constantly keep your eye open for likely prospects, no matter how improbable, including people who themselves may never have considered they might do well.

One day a PA who had been fired came in distress asking me to help find her a job. Although she had some publishing experience, it was hard work persuading her to try copywriting, but a year later she won an award and eventually became a very good creative director. Another find was someone who had been first an average receptionist, then a poor secretary and then an ill-focused art buyer before being convinced – again, with difficulty – that she might write good copy. She was a creative director in 18 months. A third was our librarian, a PhD. I asked if he liked his job and he said, 'Not particularly.' So I asked him what he'd really like to do, and he said, 'Be a writer.'

Being a writer doesn't call for massive expenditure or planning. You just find some paper and start writing. Anyhow I gave him a shot. Now he too is a highly successful creative director. Another was a radio journalist with a passion for betting on horses, which she now fulfils, I am told, by making a lot of money as a freelance.

Recently others – I think Martin Sorrell, writing in *Admap*, was one – have expressed concern about recruitment. The various schemes afoot to do something about it will no doubt throw up good executives and planners. But I doubt they will produce many good creative people, who seem to come from the oddest backgrounds. I have no recipe for success in this: just trial, error and luck. Like most people I dwell on my successes more than my mistakes but I think the prime requisite is an insatiable interest in people. And what a glorious feeling when you get it right!

NOTE: The successful librarian, Steve Harrison, is now a partner in his own agency, which does very well. Oddly enough, one of his partners also used to work with me – but I can claim no credit for his success.

□ □ □

DATE: MARCH 1997

WHY ARE YOU WRITING – AND WHAT ARE YOU SAYING?

Are you tired, irritable, overworked? Not enough hours in the day? Maybe it's because your day contains too many words – too many people chattering but saying nothing in meetings; too many people sending stuff that takes too long to get to the point, doesn't get to the point, or entirely misses the point.

Read this: 'The crucial resource which will deliver the desired business plan outcomes is, as ever, the people resource.' Doesn't that mean: 'You need good people to get good results'? The culprits are consultants called Results International. They sent me their newsletter, *The Results Bulletin*, from which I drew that exquisitely tortuous passage.

Do you really have enough time in your day to read about 'How many people buy into your Agency Vision?' (Mine has always been 'Work till lunch, then go home.')

Their thinking is quite good judging by the newsletter – but if you hire them will you have to read and listen to presentations, letters and reports that are all, like that sentence, full of jargon and twice as long as necessary? And how much will it cost you to be thus tormented?

Do you really have enough time in your day to read about 'How many people buy into your Agency Vision?' (Mine has always been 'Work till lunch, then go home.') Is there not more to life than 'detailed quantitative feedback from current clients about how you perform against their priorities'? Do I really need a Culture Audit – whether it is a priceless 'diagnostic tool' or even a 'sophisticated listening tool'? Maybe. But if they can't write concisely or well, what makes you imagine they can think properly?

Excuse such intemperate defence of the English language; but it really is a shame that people who clearly have some intelligent if not entirely new thoughts cannot express them clearly, or even answer their own questions. I turned, for example, to the back page of their bulletin. A heading read, 'Who are Results?' Since the bulletin had no accompanying letter, I wanted to know. I was thwarted.

They began: 'The birth of our Web site was not (as some may have spotted) closely followed by our Web page www.resultsconsultancy.com going live.' Then there was lots more stuff about them, but none of it much help. They have nine consultants, which is wonderful – for them, perhaps. But who **are** they, I wondered, becoming frustrated. Well, they told me what they did – vaguely; about their international network – even more vaguely; how long they've been in business; how they want to be seen by 'the industry'. But I never found out what I wanted to know: who **are** they?

As I say, all this started when they sent me the bulletin with no covering letter. Such a letter, explaining (amongst other things) who you are and your reason for writing, is essential. A startling number of marketers don't know this. But what you have just read shows what happens when a columnist with time on his hands gets such a mailing. He says things to his PA like, 'Who are they? Why have they sent this to me? What do they want?' Answers, please, in every mailing.

NOTE: Very shrewdly, the boss of the firm I was so rude about invited me to lunch and got me to write an article for him.

□ □ □

DATE: JULY 1998

NOW THAT WASN'T SUCH A GOOD IDEA, WAS IT?

Introduction

To be honest, the title of this section is a bit of a cheek. That's because, if you flick through these pages, you will soon see that one element in this book is conspicuous: dumb ideas people have had. And not just had, but carried through vigorously, at vast cost to their employers, colleagues or customers – and sometimes all three.

In fact there are so many such examples that I was tempted to call the whole book *The Annals of Marketing Folly*. But anyhow, this part features some of the more ludicrous things I've noticed over the seven years I have been writing for *Marketing*. Many have made me laugh out loud and I hope a few amuse you.

Once again, you will find that besides pointing out what – to me, anyhow – was wrong with some of the activities described, you can gather what I think is right, because if this book has one serious purpose, it is the rather old-fashioned one of not only entertaining but also instructing.

DO **YOU** TRUST YOUR EMPLOYER?

I think I once revealed in the pages of *Marketing* that I spent a morning in the 60s benefiting from the advice of the celebrated Dr Ernest Dichter. You may never have heard of him, but he was a psychologist who coined one of those jazzy phrases well calculated to have big corporations reaching for their chequebooks, thus making their progenitors much richer much faster than otherwise would have been the case.

His particular jazzy phrase was 'motivational research' and he was able, like all successful consultants, to make the trivial sound infinitely more important and deep than it is. His most famous *aperçu* was 'A convertible is like a mistress', which probably cost Ford or General Motors untold thousands. It probably also led to the popular parlour game in which customers are asked to compare a brand or firm with some animal or person.

> **I**n over 50 per cent of a selection of US organizations that had been re-engineered it did more harm than good.

I have never understood what benefit could possibly derive from this, but it can lead to hilarious results. In one case a group of staff compared their organization to a cockroach, scorpion and one or two other beasties you wouldn't care to meet close up late at night, let alone work for five days a week.

Many employees probably regard their firms in much the same light, and I don't blame them. AT&T started the year by announcing they intended to fire 40,000 employees, which had a gratifying effect upon their share price, and no doubt their chairman's bonus. When queried it emerged the figure had been plucked out of thin air because it sounded impressive, though not, I suspect, to the poor sods who'll get fired.

A lot of this has to do with pernicious theories like down-sizing, right-sizing and, a subject I have discussed before, re-engineering. Recent studies give an idea of how well these nostrums, often peddled by quacks who have rarely run anything themselves let alone risked their own money, actually work. In over 50 per cent of a selection of US organizations that had been re-engineered it did more harm than good.

One thing we can safely say about cockroaches and scorpions is that whilst they may not be very lovable, at least they are good at what they do. This is not the case with so many managements whose indecision, laziness and consequent lack of confidence often lead them to import consultants.

Some of these ramblings were prompted by the activities of Ed Carter, who you will recall has been employed by BT, no doubt at a fancy price, to tell them how to run their marketing. A shame, really. I cannot believe a business is in safe hands unless its bosses have a clear idea of what to do anyhow. That's what they're paid for. An internal survey last year revealed only a fifth of BT employees thought managers could be relied upon to do what they had said. Since in the case of the marketing department they don't have the power, this is hardly surprising.

To be fair, BT denies that Mr Carter is running the show; but I prefer to put my trust in the old and sound journalistic maxim: 'Never believe a rumour until it's denied.'

NOTE: Mr Carter was a fat American consultant so uncouth and, allegedly, physically violent that BT's advertising agency refused to have him on their premises. See 'Confused? You will be' on page 9.

□　□　□

DATE: JUNE 1996

HOW MUCH IS CHARM WORTH?

David Ogilvy once bought me dinner at Claridges. This, I learnt from one of his oldest associates, was a rare event. My informant had known him for over 30 years without ever getting him to pick up the tab.

Though I'm sure it was all paid for on his expenses, he was reassuringly true to his Scottish heritage. He was mean with the wine – a half-carafe of house red – and only bought one course (each, not between two). But, as always, he was generous with his thoughts, which I invariably find interesting, often funny and sometimes delightfully slanderous.

'Do you know the secret of success in this business?' he asked me in his sudden way. 'No,' I replied. 'Charm,' he said, in the grand bow-wow voice he reserved for revelations. I was thinking about this the other day, when considering the TV commercials for one bank I did not mention in my recent broadside on financial advertising.

> The woman has clearly had a severe charisma bypass operation, being an unpleasant person of extremely politically correct opinions.

Do commercials with charming people in them sell better? And conversely, do those featuring obnoxious prats have a deleterious effect? Awareness is the rather unsatisfactory measure generally used by advertisers. But clearly you can have a campaign with extremely high awareness that irritates the hell out of many of those who see it. The boorish antics of the unspeakable Danny Baker selling detergent come to mind, but I don't buy it very often. However, I do have a little money. So let's discuss the current commercials for the Co-operative Bank.

A typical one, as I recall, opens on a shaky close-up, somewhat distorted by the lens chosen, of a woman's left nostril, panning back to reveal the moonscape of her face, the whole shot in grainy black and white, reminiscent of a cross between early Vittorio De Sica and a very dull 1930s documentary about Hull clog-makers.

The woman has clearly had a severe charisma bypass operation, being an unpleasant person of extremely politically correct opinions – probably the 'chair' of the local wimmin's anarchist knitting circle. She speaks in the self-righteous monotone normally reserved for her speeches in that capacity, but is in fact explaining the policies of the bank. Other commercials in the series have the same ambience.

How did these commercials come about? Are people who believe in doing the right thing all would-be Islington councillors? More importantly, do such people have much money to put in banks?

The bank's proposition – we only invest in worthy things – appeals to me quite strongly. Indeed their press advertising has expressed it very well, but the style and casting of these commercials undoes the good work. They bring out my Marxist tendencies. I wouldn't join any club full of the people featured in them. Maybe it's just me, but I asked one or two other people (liberal types, also quite good bank prospects) and they seemed to agree.

Incidentally there is a puzzle at the end of the commercial. A rather different thought is introduced. Most slogans are a complete waste of time. This one, though, is excellent: 'The Co-operative Bank – why bank with one that isn't?' Unfortunately it has no obvious connection with what precedes it. I see the account is under review.

NOTE: Danny Baker was and may still be a vulgar 'cockney' comedian. The agency responsible was furious about this, and wrote, as usual ignoring the fact that I was talking about the TV commercials, to tell me how well the advertising (which was, as I pointed out, excellent) was doing. Agency people are rather like politicians. You talk about one thing; they respond to another.

□ □ □

DATE: FEBRUARY 1995

MYSTERIES BENEATH THE STREETS

You, like me, are no doubt familiar with the phrase 'a Freudian slip'. I say so because on the underground the other day I saw what I thought must be a Freudian jockstrap. It was a *Punch* poster featuring that handy piece of sporting apparel stuffed with pound notes and the line, 'If we catch you at it, you'll be in it.'

It is part of an excellent but utterly misguided campaign. All the posters are striking, witty, well designed and to the point; pictures and words work well together. But how can you take a journal like *Punch*, known for a century and a half for one thing – ie being funny, then less funny and finally downright dull – and present it as something utterly different, an investigative journal?

I reckon sheep on drugs must have dreamt up CNN's new effort: two words, 'Vantage Point', plus the brand name, and lots of lines like map contours.

The only time I recall such a repositioning succeeding was with Marlboro cigarettes in the 1950s. They were originally aimed at women but transformed to become a symbol of machismo. This was only possible because they hadn't had time to have a strong identity; but *Punch* does – and it is not as an investigative journal. Very odd, because the owner of *Punch* is famous for, amongst other things, claiming to have swapped wads of dough for favours from MPs. It is hard to believe this does not pop into the mind of anyone reasonably well informed who sees one of these posters, which are all on the same theme, and cause a fleeting smile, if not a belly laugh.

This leads me to something I covered the other week – posters. I was discussing roadside posters; but unlike most of **them**, underground posters may be seen for several minutes, or even, the way the tube is running lately, half an hour. Anyhow, that means you can say quite a lot on them and it is interesting to see how people exploit, or more often don't exploit, this. A perfect poster for John Lewis says, 'If John Lewis is never knowingly undersold, why aren't our carpets the cheapest you can buy?' There follows lots of elegantly laid out copy, well calculated to persuade most people that John Lewis give you a better deal for your money, even if they aren't always the cheapest.

Others examples puzzle me. I reckon sheep on drugs must have dreamt up CNN's new effort: two words, 'Vantage Point', plus the brand name, and lots of lines like map contours. Almost incomprehensible; and even when you work out what they're driving at, it's obvious that any competitor – the BBC, ITN, NBC – could make the same point just as credibly. Amerada – believe it or not, a gas company – show a dull diagram of a house, captioned 'a global gas company you can now fit in your home' plus the fatuous slogan, 'Amerada – fuel for thought'. The thought it fuelled in me was: why should I try Amerada? The answer came almost instantly, because I saw over someone's shoulder an excellent editorial-style ad saying, 'Amerada raises standards and lowers bills.' Why did nobody have the wit to use that or something similar on the posters? It's a mystery.

□ □ □

DATE: APRIL 1998

NEVER MIND THE STRATEGY; WHAT ABOUT THE RESULTS?

Do you recall the people who influenced you most? Rufus Leven, a copywriter I worked with in 1960 in Manchester, made a vast impression on me.

For one thing, although he was 50 and nothing special to look at, he lived with a beautiful girl of 19, which I thought amazing and altogether admirable. For another, he was a former member of the Central Committee of the Communist Party of Great Britain, having been born a rich sprig of the family that made Markovitch Black and White cigarettes.

When he became a communist he changed his name to Ron to sound more working class. We used to spend hours talking about his life, and he told me enough about politics to persuade me to give up my ambition to become prime minister by the age of 30, and enough about the real world to distrust most experts and all authority.

> The word 'strategy', of course, derives from the Greek for 'general', but the best generals were less concerned with strategy than more practical matters.

I recalled him fondly the other day when I found a copy of John Donne's sonnets he had inscribed to me. Around the same time he introduced me to another very different book, Claud Cockburn's hilarious autobiography. Cockburn, also once a communist, was one of the people behind *Private Eye*, which was partly inspired by a scurrilous publication he ran in the 30s called *The Week* – unrelated to the excellent journal of that title today.

Cockburn had been Washington correspondent of *The Times* and, earlier, a sub-editor. In his book he told a funny story about a contest the subs ran for the dullest heading of the day. I seem to recall he won with 'Small earthquake in Chile. Not many dead.' His spirit would take its hat off, I suspect, to the main heading on the front page of *Marketing* a while ago: 'ICL unifies core brand strategy.'

In some ways this is better than his Chilean line. Besides being stupefyingly dull (surely **something** interesting occurred in marketing that week) it is quite meaningless to anyone who does not delve in the recondite corners where reports are written in this business, and nigh on incomprehensible even to one who does.

The word 'strategy', of course, derives from the Greek for 'general', but the best generals were less concerned with strategy than more practical matters. Marlborough arranged for his troops to have fresh boots just before his greatest victory, Blenheim. The military book that influenced Napoleon most was not about strategy. It was *Essay on Tactics* by the Comte de Guibert. Conversely, *War and Peace* records that the Austrian and Russian armies Napoleon wiped the floor with at Austerlitz were following 'the new science of strategics'. Wellington, who finally beat Napoleon, when asked for the secret of his success, replied, 'Attention to detail.'

You will have noticed that outside factors, aided by our government's clever spending policies, are leading to a recession. When it comes, will it be enough to unify your core brand strategy? Maybe you can fool people with that sort of stuff for a while, but eventually results will be required, which is one reason why economic storms are rather salutary. They remind us that marketing, like war, is about simple, practical things, not pretentious verbal frippery.

NOTE: As so often in these columns, I was wrong about the recession arriving. Despite the government's efforts, it has not come yet; but I will be right when it does.

□ □ □

DATE: SEPTEMBER 1998

NOT A VERY GOOD IDEA

Who says there's no such thing as a free lunch? The publishers of this esoteric organ bought me one at the Marketing Society's annual Christmas bash. The speaker was Michael Heseltine. Making such speeches used to be easy, he said. You just rang Conservative Central Office's jokes department for some timely quips. Unfortunately it had been closed down.

I could have shown him a good marketing joke: the big illuminated sign on the Battersea Power Station, reading 'Midland 97'. This 'initiative' came about after the Midland Bank announced it was to stop sponsoring opera as too 'elitist'. Instead they funded 17 days of pre-Christmas jollity featuring the likes of Boyzone, Morrissey and the Brand New Heavies. I tried to picture how this came about. Perhaps some sleek, corpulent Tai-pan from the Hong Kong and Shanghai Bank – new owners of the Midland – was advised that they should go for the 'youth market'. Or – who knows? – maybe a 'communications strategist' said, 'Research says we're still known as the "listening bank". Deafening everyone for miles will play off our existing imagery.'

Dopey proposals always find a welcome in the marble halls of bloated institutions.

But what did this achieve? Did it lift awareness (costliest word in the marketer's vocabulary)? Impossible, surely. If anyone in Britain hasn't heard of the Midland, I'll be hornswoggled. It certainly did them no good amongst their neighbours, who were infuriated by the din. In my block the management committee put up a sign suggesting any Midland customers complain to their bank manager, and giving a phone number everyone else could call.

To add to their misfortunes, they attracted so few people they had to abolish admission charges. But what of those who did turn up? What is the aftermath of a couple of hours of the tedious Morrissey? You can picture the conversations. 'What should we do, love? Switch the overdraft to the Midland or go home and throw up?' Do Boyzone induce any feeling, except that BoysIIMen did the same thing four years earlier and twice as well?

To score one own goal is a misfortune; to score two takes real dedication. How would a sensible bank have viewed this silly venture? Take one that is making big inroads in this country – MBNA. I picture them as a bunch of flinty-eyed mid-westerners, though they're probably nothing of the sort. Imagine the derisive hoots of laughter ringing through their conference rooms if someone suggested this silly idea. I imagine they'd ask pointed questions. Can you justify this? What measurable results will it produce? How many new cards will we get? How many new customers? How rich are Boyzone fans compared to the folks we'll enrage in Chelsea? Followed by, 'Get out of here with that dumb idea.'

'Prosperity doth best discover vice, but adversity doth best discover virtue,' wrote Francis Bacon. The better firms do, the harder they find it to behave sensibly. Dopey proposals always find a welcome in the marble halls of bloated institutions. The Midland–Hong Kong conglomerate is currently the world's largest bank, though two Swiss monsters are joining to create a bigger one. Is this wise? Intelligence and common sense are more often the prerogative of the small and nimble. Big is rarely beautiful – or smart.

□ □ □

DATE: JANUARY 1998

90

STYLE NO SUBSTITUTE FOR SUBSTANCE

I told you a while ago that the Cable & Wireless mob would spend ages footling about with their 'corporate image' instead of getting down to their jobs. Soon they'll start the usual silly advertising campaign – aimed at themselves, of course, because no one else gives a hoot – about whatever they think they have now miraculously become. I'll bet a fiver to a bent tin can it will be a deluge of aren't-we-clever old tosh.

The RAC are engaged in a similar but even more asinine exercise, 'restyling' themselves in what Gavin Stamp in *The Spectator* accurately describes as 'so often the action of an institution in decline – by dropping the royal crown and adopting a peculiarly hideous and outdated sans-serif logo'. The value of the word 'royal' has always been such that its use has been hedged about, rightly, with great restrictions. These fools have given it up, no doubt because some research says people don't esteem our royal family as they did. They are wrong. Thousands of years of engrained respect for the idea of monarchy do not vanish in 10 years because a few idiots in two generations of one uncannily stupid family behave foolishly.

> **How many marketers, if they were to reach the happy circumstance of having an entire product named after their region, would willingly give it up?**

Which reminds me: the New Zealanders, you may have read, have decided to 'rename' the kiwi fruit and call it the 'zespri' because too many 'low price producers' are eating into their market – forgive the pun. I can understand rebranding, but not renaming. Is it possible to change the way most people describe a well-known product without spending years and millions? I doubt it. Is it wise? It sounds downright dumb to me. The kiwi fruit has another name already anyhow – the 'Chinese gooseberry'. But how many marketers, if they were to reach the happy circumstance of having an entire product named after their region, would willingly give it up, let alone seek to? Surely it is close to being a marketer's nirvana. Would the Champenois want to change the name champagne? *Au contraire*: they wisely spent fortunes making it illegal for anyone else to use it. Camembert, Brie and Cheddar folk should have but didn't, poor things.

Here are a couple of analogies. How much do you imagine it is worth to Hoover for 'Hoover' to be the word people use all over the world when describing machines that clean carpets? Despite Hoover's listless marketing, how long did it take Electrolux and Vax to overtake them? What is it worth to Xerox for people everywhere to apply their brand name to all copying? How much has it cost people like Canon to steal part of their market? Xerox were there first, and still remain well placed despite some very odd decisions, like throwing away the extraordinary advantage of inventing the first PC. The kiwi fruit analogy is not exactly on all fours but the New Zealanders are in the glorious position of having an entire product named after their country. They should exploit it, not throw it away.

Marketers move in mysterious ways their wonders to perform, don't they? Maybe that's why so many don't succeed.

□ □ □

DATE: MAY 1997

THE MISUSE OF LANGUAGE

As you get older you notice to your chagrin that you're starting to show some of the traits of your parents, especially those you found most odious.

My father, who ran a pub, was what they call 'a character' – a valuable attribute, since many customers came just to marvel at his antics. But these were often less fun for us. Being miserly, he used to go round the kitchen regularly turning down the gas cookers – no help if you're trying to serve meals on time. And he had a filthy temper, to gratify which he used to turn on the wireless each morning and wait to hear a singer he didn't like, just for the pleasure of snapping 'yowling bitch' and turning it off.

> Why do people speak such tripe? I suppose it makes them feel better about themselves. Ordinary people now talk about images and brand values.

I am becoming increasingly intolerant myself about things that don't matter. The other day I read an interview with an agency boss. Deftly combining cliché and inaccuracy, he said of his love for wine: 'It's a great conversation-starter. Also it helps to know your Beaujolais from the rest of your Burgundies.' 'But not as much as if you know Beaujolais **isn't** a Burgundy,' I muttered pettishly.

I'm like someone scratching an itch: I can't help analysing such claptrap. When Fergie said she was going to 'down-shift her lifestyle', I wondered irritably how it could get much lower than it was and why she didn't just say she was going to squander less money. Reading a man's description of his life's work as 'providing Internet and Intranet communications to the corporate environment', I wondered what he meant. And if he meant what I think, was it true? Suppose the Sultan of Brunei offered him £10 million for a basinful of Internet and Intranet. Would this chap turn him down because he isn't a corporation?

The evidence suggests management consultants have now overtaken marketers as world champions of linguistic garbage. 'We deal with the nuts and bolts, but we cannot work in a vacuum – our work must be viewed holistically. Some of our guys have marketing experience – but this does not play to our core skills. Basically, our remit is always to change a department's functioning so that it is more effective and more efficient,' prattles Ann Ross of Andersen Consulting. William L Shulby of Ernst & Young babbles, 'We have involvement with the top executives in the company. We think issues through with them; we set up their success requirements and build key matrices. If you don't have this communication with the management – the sponsorship from the top if you like – you will sub-optimize the results of the exercise.' Pick the bones out of that lot.

Why do people speak such tripe? I suppose it makes them feel better about themselves. It certainly impresses the gullible. What worries me is that it is wildly contagious. Ordinary people now talk about images and brand values. Eventually it will be impossible to have an intelligible conversation. I must proactively realign my key issues, refurbish my mission statement and re-engineer my core competences – before it's too late.

□ □ □

DATE: APRIL 1997

THE TROUBLE WITH MARKETING

Here's how you presented the ads 37 years ago when I wrote copy for Imperial Leather. You read them to the sister of the firm's boss and then showed her the layouts. You did it bolt upright on a small, uncomfortable chair in a little room. If you were lucky she OKed them.

It worked, too. More people buy Imperial Leather today than any other soap. But I thought the process was ridiculous. I wanted to be judged by the customers, not the clients, so I went into direct marketing. But that story is the prelude for some serious comment because, despite all the hoopla and pseudo-intellectual guff pervading our industry, I doubt whether many people do better today than that (very shrewd) lady did then.

> **Y**ou can see why marketers are poorly thought of. Bizarrely for people involved in communications, few write well; fewer are broadly cultured; hardly any study their profession.

Sadly, our industry media, including this magazine, too often hold up for admiration the most dreadful people – bullies, and smoke-and-mirror merchants – whose chief skills are adroit self-promotion and polysyllabic waffle. They float between overpaid, fancy-titled jobs for years before being found out. Some move so fast their misdeeds never catch up with them.

Writing rude pieces is fun, but what is the solution? The hirers are the reason phoneys are hired. Education, as usual, is the answer, starting at the top. How many senior directors of disasters like W H Smith or Sears understand marketing? Have they noticed or learnt from the fact that their best competitors – entrepreneurs like Branson or Murdoch, and firms like Unilever or Procter & Gamble – are brilliant at it?

Effectiveness awards do much good, but are their lessons publicized enough in the right places? Ed Artzt, P & G's ex-chairman, once remarked that they measure everything. That is vital, too – proper measurement, not unscientific guesswork based on statistically unrepresentative focus groups. Often the measurement is naïve or pointless. What do you learn from knowing how much various firms spent on ads last week? Or from which campaigns were most recalled? The two figures must be linked to have any meaning.

You can see why marketers are poorly thought of. Bizarrely for people involved in communications, few write well; fewer are broadly cultured; hardly any study their profession (or trade, as I would say) deeply. Frankly, I can understand why. Most serious business books are dreary and ill written. Those that aren't – Sloan, Ogilvy, Townsend, Reeves, for instance – are rarely read.

Frankly, it's disgraceful how little training there is in our industry. Young people come to us barely literate or numerate; many 'creatives' don't seem to appreciate that marketing is about selling. And what do we do about it? Far too little. This may not be true of your firm, but it is of most, believe me.

Marketing is like management consultancy – immature, and maybe worse. 'How do I know if McKinsey & Co are the world's best?' asks a former AT&T employee in the new book *Dangerous Company* (O'Shea and Madigan, 1997). 'What businesses have they managed? Look at the people they send out, all under 30 and fresh out of business school.'

Trouble is, most of our lot haven't even been to business school.

□ □ □

DATE: DECEMBER 1997

THIS WEEK, A LITTLE HISTORY FOR YOU

'When I survey life, 'tis all a cheat; yet fooled by hope, we favour the deceit,' wrote Dryden. I must be a gloomy old sod, because I agree with his sentiments. How could human beings survive some of the crap they have to put up with but for optimism?

Take the way we fondly confuse progress with change. I was told recently that the Incas taxed their subjects by making them work for three months a year for nothing. The Incas were clever people: they may not have been familiar with the idea of the wheel, but their work-tax produced some of the most remarkable and beautiful edifices ever known. Ours pay for farces like the Millennium Dome and a ceaseless torrent of regulations stopping us doing what we want to do, or protecting us from the consequences.

> People remember successful advertising campaigns long after they have ceased to run.

Maybe the Incas were rather better at managing things than our governments, too. Our high level of tax means we work for the government not for three, but nigh on six months a year.

I was not around, despite what some of my friends think, at the time of the Incas, but I have been in this business for quite a few years. My overwhelming impression is that marketing people not only confuse change with progress, but they also have absolutely no awareness of the past.

Contrary to the belief amongst the naïve, 'Times change; people don't', as someone wiser than me once put it. That which was a good idea 50 or even 100 years ago is likely to be a good idea today; and that which was a dumb idea then is likely to be just as dumb now. Thirty years ago, people discovered what a stupid idea Green Shield Stamps were. Now they are embracing the folly of that approach again, but this time it has been tarted up as 'loyalty programmes'.

Goodness knows how much time, trouble and money could be saved if people studied history a little. One person, Robin Wight, has made it an important element in his rather brilliant career. For years he has recommended to clients what he calls advertising archaeology. He points out something we all know: people remember successful advertising campaigns long after they have ceased to run. So it's worth looking at what's worked well for you in the past and seeing if you shouldn't resuscitate it.

There are two admirable things about this approach. First, recycling old ideas that have worked is a lot easier, and could well be more reliable, than finding new ones that may not work. And second, old advertising is not just of historic interest: it represents money, money invested in creating a brand. When you move away from it you are, as it were, throwing away the benefits of your investment.

There is a very good exposition of Robin's views on this and related matters in *Forensic Marketing*, a book edited and partly written by Gavin Barrett, but now out of print. It is a compendium of articles by various luminaries, and it contains some good stuff, some on matters unwisely neglected, like 'below-the-line' (stupid phrase) literature. What he means is that all the messages, about service and the like, are ones that marketers tend to feel are too trivial to spend a lot of time or thought on, but which matter so much to customers. Too many people in our business mistake the visible for the important.

□ □ □

DATE: DECEMBER 1998

98

WHICH ARE THE MODELS TO EMULATE?

Having spent 40-odd years learning, with great difficulty, to write, I was torn between hysteria and derision when I read that 'supermodel' Christie Turlington is going to write a book, following the lead of the traffic-stopping Naomi. However her agent says she is very serious about it, even going as far as 'taking classes to be told what to read'.

She shows a most laudable self-discipline; and I shall approach the late-blossoming career as a model that I am now planning in the same spirit. But hard work is quite the fashion in modelling. In a 1994 interview Cindy Crawford asked, 'Do you think I look like this naturally? I work. I work eight hours a day to look like this.' This is an attitude many in our field would laugh to scorn, preferring the sloth's gospel of 'Express thyself' to applying proboscis to grindstone.

> **M**arketing is not a matter of life and death; but I find it interesting that the people I admire most have been, without exception, keen students.

I cannot think of any serious business where not some but most of the people take so little trouble to study. It is not the exception but the rule that, when at conferences or seminars I ask who has read one of the cardinal works on the subject, *Ogilvy on Advertising* (1987), a tiny minority raise their hands. No wonder so few can write: hardly any of them have read. How, then, can we be surprised at the constant stream of speeches and articles on the theme of 'Whither – if anywhere – marketing?' Imagine if doctors were let loose on their patients with so little knowledge.

Marketing is not a matter of life and death; but I find it interesting that the people I admire most have been, without exception, keen students.

David Ogilvy once confided to me that he had stolen everything he knew from John Caples, and that his brother-in-law Rosser Reeves admitted the same. Anyone who has not read Caples on *How to Make Your Advertising Make Money* (1983) or *Tested Advertising Methods* (1997) certainly should.

I used to read the latter repeatedly, as I did Ogilvy's *Confessions* (1963), Reeves' *Reality in Advertising* (out of print) and, of course, the shortest and probably the best book on the subject ever written, *Scientific Advertising* by Claude Hopkins, published in 1924. Ogilvy observed of it: 'Nobody at any level should be allowed to have anything to do with advertising until he has read this book seven times. Every time I see a bad advertisement, I say to myself, "The man who wrote this copy has never read Claude Hopkins."' Unfortunately the book is now out of print. I stole my copy from Ken Roman, former head of the Ogilvy Group, who himself has co-written an excellent book called *How to Advertise* (Roman and Maas, 1976).

But when we consider our audience perhaps all this study is wasted. The other day I was riffling through the *Sunday People* magazine. I saw a heading that read: 'Win £100.' Beneath was a picture of a shapely rump in a bikini bottom. The copy read: 'Can you tell us what this mystery object is? It's taken from a picture on page 40.' I boggled. 'Looks a lot like an arse to me,' I muttered to myself.

I turned to page 40. It was an arse. Ah, the joys of the consumer society.

NOTE: This was written at a time when it looked as though 'models' were about to take over the world. The spectacularly lovely Naomi Campbell had written – or had had written for her – a spectacularly bad novel. Unlike her, it flopped.

□ □ □

DATE: SEPTEMBER 1995

So You Want to be Creative

Introduction

As far as I can judge, everyone loves to be seen as creative, or at least as associated with the creative act. This comes out in advertising and marketing journals where sycophantic pieces refer to the marketing director of some firm or another as the person 'behind' or 'responsible for' some famous commercial or advertising campaign.

You can be quite sure that the same marketing director will have boasted to his pals about the wonderful new commercials his firm is running. Usually you can be equally sure that he had nothing to do with the campaign. He was sold it by some smooth talkers from his agency, and then took the credit after it ran. Nine times out of 10 the agency people will practically have had to strangle him to get him to approve it.

In the world's creativity charts of advertising – the various award schemes that run in exotic spots like Cannes – British advertising has an extraordinarily good record. We punch above our weight – which makes it all the more surprising that so much creative work is so bad, and so few people understand what makes for good work.

BULLYING WIVES AND SILK UNDERWEAR

Composers, like everyone else, come in all shapes and sizes. Hitler's favourite, Richard Strauss, was a tiny man who by a satisfying compensatory mechanism wrote some of the loudest music for the biggest orchestras ever. I suppose the piece even the least musical among us recognize is *Also Sprach Zarathustra* – the theme for *2001: Space Odyssey*.

His wife, who clearly had a touch of *der Führer* about her would instruct him every morning, with admirable simplicity: 'Richard, go compose!' and then send him to his work room – a disciplined approach to the act of creation, you will agree, and not unlike Anthony Trollope's. He worked for the Post Office, writing his novels in the mornings, starting at 5.30.

> The solution was to lock him in a room with two bottles of claret, a pen, ink and limitless writing paper. I have found two of the elements in that solution effective myself.

To grind out his interminable masterpieces Wagner demanded the most sumptuous conditions – incense, silk underwear and rich fabrics. Rossini found writing so easy he banged out *Il Barbiere di Seviglia* in 13 days, a celerity put to shame by Donizetti, who dashed off *L'Elisir d'Amour* in eight. That was because he always left things to the last minute, an approach most of us can relate to with ease. The playwright Sheridan's last-ditch tactics were so extreme that two days before the opening night of *The Rivals* he had not started the last act. His backers were understandably rather agitated. The solution was to lock him in a room with two bottles of claret, a pen, ink and limitless writing paper. I have found two of the elements in that solution effective myself.

There seems to be no relationship between the methods used and the quality of the work, save that they were all writing under some sort of pressure, whether to eat, keep the wife quiet, or justify, in Wagner's case, the ruinous amount of money he cost Ludwig of Bavaria – who went mad, quite understandably.

In our business we too are under pressure to produce ideas. Only one person I know of has systematically explained the process in a way ordinary people can understand: James Webb Young, a brilliant early creative director of J Walter Thompson, New York, in a book called *A Technique for Producing Ideas* (reprinted 1988).

Here's a rather free summary of what he learnt, which starts, not surprisingly, with learning everything about what you are selling and the people you are selling to: what they like, what they want, their hopes, dreams, fears. Next, let your mind roam free – to explore the possibilities. Dismiss nothing that occurs to you, no matter how silly or seemingly irrelevant.

The critical step is perhaps the next one: you just put the problem aside and relax. Ideas, which you sometimes feel come inexplicably from thin air, often originate in your subconscious mind, which seems to need this relaxing process to work best. As the deadline nears, return to the task.

A grasp of technique is essential, clearly. Always overwrite and then cut, not vice versa. Apart from being able to write properly, you must know how to persuade. You start by making a proposition people find easy to accept, before leading them through a series of other, less plausible ones, until the final request for action seems perfectly reasonable.

Oh, and for God's sake, edit, edit, edit.

☐ ☐ ☐

DATE: MAY 1996

DRIVING CUSTOMERS TO DESPAIR

Having read the *Mail on Sunday* describing Paul Gascoigne as a 'tormented genius', I think I'll get stinking drunk, go home, kick the dog, strangle the cat and beat the living shit out of the wife. If that's what it takes to be a genius, I'll make the sacrifice. I've always agreed with whoever said genius was an infinite capacity for taking pains. Apparently, though, it's an infinite capacity for giving them.

Mind you, I've never had illusions about my genius, if such a word could, however remotely, be used in the context of our business. My performance has often been so pathetic I have nightmares just thinking about it. For instance, in 1966 I did the launch advertising for the Audi. My God, it was bad, though in some ways no worse than some recent ads.

> **S**ome advertising people suffer from the bizarre delusion that customers are as entranced by advertising as they are.

For Honda the creative people fall back on a pun, with the headline, 'A press ad for the Honda Civic'. How we could mistake it for anything else I can't think. It didn't resemble a pterodactyl, a King Charles spaniel, an article on 20th-century philosophy or a recipe for fried chicken. In fact it showed pictures of the buttons you can press when you buy a Honda, which look to me just like the buttons you can press on other cars. To my mind a weak play on words is no substitute for saying something relevant and competitive that makes me feel I would prefer a Honda to anything else available.

Things are not much better when we turn on the haunted goldfish bowl. The current Fiat commercial is an odd mishmash. First some evocative old

Italian music is played over sepia pictures – perfect if you want prospects to think Fiats are Italian but obsolete. Fighting this visually is something we are all getting rather bored with: features listed on a computer screen. When we have disentangled ourselves from these two messages to conclude whatever we are supposed to about the car, up pops one of those pretentious little lines copywriters adore – 'a choice, not a compromise'. Like most such lines this is not at all persuasive, and could be applied to almost anything; and, as with Honda, this ad promotes features, not benefits.

Some advertising people suffer from the bizarre delusion that customers are as entranced by advertising as they are, as demonstrated in the beautiful campaign for the new Audi A3, which 'doesn't need avalanches, lightning, steel spikes or walls of fire to make it look good'. Extraordinary. Rather than compare the car with other cars, they compare other car's advertising with their advertising. This may sell to a tiny deranged group who buy cars based on the creative awards the ads win, but why should it appeal to anyone else? Very sad for a brand which year after year has done fine advertising. Mind you, they prospered despite my early efforts, so they'll probably survive this too.

In all three campaigns, technique triumphs over content; not enough, I fear, in an overcrowded market like this.

□ □ □

DATE: FEBRUARY 1997

EVALUATING CREATIVE

This is the third in a series of pieces on getting your creative right. The first concerned execution, the second briefing. This is about correct evaluation.

I once asked my client, Victor Ross, then chairman of *Reader's Digest*, how well he could predict results. 'I get it right about half the time,' he said. Modest of him, I suspect, since shortly after he won a bet with me about two ads we were running. Both did badly, which neither of us expected, and that shows just how hard it is to judge creative work. However, here are five guidelines.

First, has the objective been met? Look at the brief. You may find it is inadequate, or has been ignored. However, assuming it is good, you can see whether the communication matches its objective. For instance, you don't need a four-page letter and a brochure to get a simple enquiry, whereas you will need a very elaborate confection indeed to sell something expensive.

> **S**how the work to someone who knows nothing about the job, ideally a likely prospect who is not too bright.

Second, don't waste time pondering over minutiae like the cropping of the illustration on the back of the brochure or the choice of adjectives in the letter. Is there a good idea, one that fits the positioning of your brand or product, and will attract and engage interest in a relevant way? Make sure it **is** one idea and not seven. One simple idea properly carried through will do better than several, however good, that fight with each other. That confuses your customer.

Third, remember you are not the prospect. It is hard for marketing people to know what will appeal to their customers, who do not spend their time in smart restaurants talking to obsequious advertising agencies about strategy, and are concerned about important things like their families, the outrageous price of beer and the likely winner of the FA Cup.

Fourth, does it get to the point fast? People don't wish to exert themselves following the labyrinthine musings of copywriters. Is there a clear competitive advantage, with the offer and benefit impossible to miss? Or are these buried under layers of creative self-indulgence? Settle for simple, straightforward executions rather than clever, entertaining ones (of course, if you can combine the two you really have a winner).

Fifth, is it crystal clear? Show the work to someone who knows nothing about the job, ideally a likely prospect who is not too bright. Do they understand what you are **selling**, why they should reply – and how they should reply, which should be as easy as possible? Do they think it's a good deal? Has every sensible reason for replying been given, and every reasonable objection overcome?

If you cover all five factors above, you will have done a deal better than most people who evaluate creative work – and your profits will reflect it.

NOTE: Looking through these pieces, I see some names occur more than once, for example, David Ogilvy, Leo Burnett and, here, Victor Ross. These repetitions simply reflect these people's influence on marketing, advertising – and me.

□ □ □

DATE: AUGUST 1993

FIRST THE VICES, NOW THE SINS

Some weeks ago I wrote about the five vices that lead to poor creative. Unfortunately I omitted to mention the main cause of disaster: poor briefs. Many briefs are not planned, but are the hapless offspring of hurried phone calls or late night bursts of inspiration in bars, which are transmuted into documents by fuddled account-handlers the next day. No wonder so few are good.

The first deadly sin in briefing is not explaining the context. Why are you trying to achieve your objective? Good creative minds see things you might miss, and look at your problem from a different perspective. They can often suggest a different solution. But they need to know the background.

> **A**s a young copywriter, I placed a sign over my desk reading: 'Do you want it good – or do you want it quick?'

The second sin is not allowing enough time. As a young copywriter, I placed a sign over my desk reading: 'Do you want it good – or do you want it quick?' True, there never is enough time, but you can steal time by talking regularly to your agency about what's coming up. Thus they can start mulling over ideas in advance, rather than going through the usual nightmare – the job requested on the Thursday before the Monday when you want the work.

Some time ago when judging the internal creative awards for GUS, I chose as the winner one composed of elements of a number of mailings that had worked to a greater or lesser degree in the previous seven years. This brings me to the third sin: not revealing what has worked – or failed – previously. One needs to see creative samples and know whom the work was aimed at. It's particularly valuable to know which types of people were most or least responsive.

The next sin is failure to supply competitive examples. How can you win if you don't know what you have to beat? The only time most agencies analyse the competition is to sell their ideas by comparison when pitching for the business – after which everybody neglects this tedious, but necessary review, returning thankfully to the petty urgencies of a business driven by detail.

The final sin I lay more at the door of agencies than clients. It is the passive approach – simply accepting the client's brief and starting work without going back to ask supplementary questions. Often this is because the agency is frightened to confess it didn't really understand what the client wanted. Equally often, the result is one of those dreadful meetings where the agency produces ideas which they have persuaded themselves are brilliant, only to have the client gaze at them, mystified, saying, 'This isn't what I asked for.'

Incidentally, if anyone is interested, I have a 27-point checklist covering what I think a brief should cover. Unfortunately, I suspect it is incomplete, but it's the best I've been able to come up with so far.

NOTE: Quite true: my list now contains 31 points.

□ □ □

DATE: JULY 1993

GOD BLESS YOU, SIR JOHN

If you're in bed with the flu, as I was before Christmas, any good cheer is welcome – even if only in a TV commercial. So with what joy I saw some kindly souls had pressed into service my very favourite moment of television.

I have been telling friends about it for years. It was, I believe, the last scene in the biographical series about the late John Betjeman, when his interviewer asked him if he had, looking back on his life, any regrets. 'I haven't had enough sex,' was his lugubrious reply, which the commercial – for Sekonda Watches – managed to link fittingly and elegantly to the thought that time may be precious, but need not be expensive.

> **Who, sober, could have written it? Did anybody with even a glancing knowledge of the visual arts come anywhere near it?**

Some oddball suggested the other week in these columns that this was dubbed (which it wasn't) and blasphemous. I thought it funny, unexpected, honest and oddly moving, whilst deflating, in the kindliest way, the earnestness of the questioner. In short, it combined uniquely in a phrase five elements, any one of which is rarely found in whole programmes. Raymond Rubicam once said an outstanding advertisement should not only sell, but also 'be an admirable piece of work in its own right'. To me that commercial meets the criterion perfectly.

Maledictions, though, should descend on whoever concocted the piece of boastful tosh on which Sedgwick squandered thousands in *The Economist* late last November. It featured an indifferent sketch of Mozart, whose financial skills we all recall so vividly, waving a conductor's baton, which I think had yet to be introduced in his day, over the heading 'GREAT EUROPEANS – a series from Sedgwick – No 1 in Europe'. This was set in white on an ugly grey patterned background, with the wise objective – bearing in mind the dire, self-congratulatory copy – of reducing readability as far as possible.

Even in *The Economist*, full as it is of goofy messages from obscure Slovakian and Ukrainian banks telling lies about privatization, this was outstandingly bad. Who, sober, could have written it? Did anybody with even a glancing knowledge of the visual arts come anywhere near it? Was it really approved by a sane, thinking human being?

In my first year as a copywriter, I recall with shame writing something half as bad about a new airport somewhere, but at least it only appeared in the local Liverpool paper, not a respected international journal; and I did have the excuse of youth and insufficient guidance. The silly heading suggests Sedgwick plan to repeat this sort of thing. They would do better to take the money and put it in the Lottery, whence at least they would have some chance, no matter how small, of getting a return on their investment.

Talking of which, did you know the market capitalization of Coca-Cola now stands at over $90 billion more than American Express, Disney and Motorola combined – which between them have three times the sales and 60 per cent more net income? I don't know what this says about the decline of the brand, but it certainly suggests to me that no matter how stupid we marketing people may be, we're paragons of logic compared to the stock market.

NOTE: A reader kindly pointed out to me afterwards that another watch company, not Sekonda, dragged dear old Betjeman back from the grave. This neatly demonstrates two facts often ignored. One: your advertising, especially if you use famous people, should never overshadow your product. Two: a statement that could apply equally well to any of your competitors is usually a bad idea.

□ □ □

DATE: JANUARY 1996

GOOD, BAD AND INDIFFERENT

I am usually a little disturbed when the public's opinion coincides with my own; it makes me question their judgement – or mine. But an exception occurred a while ago when in a poll by one of the music magazines Marvin Gaye's *What's Going On* was voted the greatest pop record ever made. Quite right.

What is the best commercial ever? I think it was for Volkswagen in the 60s. Like the opening of Orson Welles' *A Touch of Evil* it is one long shot. A pair of feet emerge in close-up from the door of a car and land in deep snow. The camera slowly pulls back as they crunch through the snow, until the last shot reveals a Volkswagen Beetle next to a snowplough. One wonderfully under-stated line is then delivered: 'Have you ever wondered how the man who drives the snowplough gets to the snowplough?' A striking demonstration of what sold Volkswagen: reliability – and why Doyle, Dane, Bernbach, New York was then perhaps the world's best agency.

> You can reasonably divide advertisements into four kinds: good ideas well done; good ideas badly done; bad ideas well done; and bad ideas badly done.

You can reasonably divide advertisements into four kinds: good ideas well done; good ideas badly done; bad ideas well done; and bad ideas badly done. In the last category I would put a recent poster campaign for Ruddles, whose previous effort featuring obscure jokes about Rutland I questioned – but it was better than this. Perhaps you saw it: a rather nasty blue representation of a computer screen, with lines like: Forget.e-mails. Drink. Wth. Fe/males. Not. 4 boffins//4.people.with.best.friends.

Is this any way to sell a hearty rustic brew? I entirely accept that ad agency posers spend all day tossing off in front of flickering screens but beg leave to doubt that the typical real-ale swiller does. In fact research I saw last year strongly suggests that most have no idea what e-mail is. Maybe the stuff is trotting out of the brewery by the hogshead as a result, but I simply can't believe it. There is no attempt to convey any of the important things about beer: taste, looks, strength, refreshment and glorious, seam-splitting repletion.

Conversely, I thought another recent campaign, for Colman's English mustard, was a good idea well done, with just the sort of language and humour Ruddles should be using. There's only one good thing you can say about Colman's unique aid to digestion: it blows your stomach apart. This campaign says so, with jovial yokels delivering lines like: 'Smite my grunions with a spreckle rake! That Colman's is what I call a mustard and a half' and 'Frettle my welters! That Colman's has more kick than a mule in a bramble bush.' I'm not sure how much life the product has left in it, but those ads will bring it out if anything can.

The difference between these two campaigns for me is that one shows understanding of the customer and the other doesn't. And as Harvey MacKay observes in *Swim with the Sharks without being Eaten Alive* (1989), something you know about your customer may be more important than anything you know about your product.

□ □ □

DATE: SEPTEMBER 1996

HOW LONG, O LORD, HOW LONG?

We're all familiar with those philosophical disputes conducted amongst the more retarded members of society which go rather like: 'Man United is the best f—ing football team in the f—ing country.' 'No it f—ing isn't.' 'Yes it f—ing is' – and so on.

Such exchanges represent the very acme of logic compared with what I read a few weeks ago in *Campaign*, where it seems, dear readers, that otherwise quite bright people have been seeking – yet again – the answer to the timeless problem: 'How long should copy be?' And if there were a Museum of the Moronic, some of the views expressed definitely deserve a proud

> **I**f it's interesting people will read a lot, whereas if it's boring they'll read none.

place there. No less a personage than John Hegarty of BBH magisterially stated, 'Long copy is an indulgence.' I can't believe anyone as wise and god-like really made such a bizarre remark, and trust he was either misquoted or recovering from a good lunch. If not, I shall have to recast him as the Michael Heseltine of advertising. But there he was in black and white, abetted by Patrick Collister, creative director of O & M, who suggested 'Literacy is irrelevant' nowadays.

Discussing the length of copy is as futile as wondering how tall a good general should be. However, if any reader should be fooled by the first statement above, it has been well and wittily rebutted by two friends of mine. One, the creative director of O & M, New Delhi, replied: 'How much string do you need to wrap a parcel?' The other, Bill Jayme, the world's highest paid direct mail copywriter (up to $40,000 a mailing), said: 'Nobody ever complained that *Gone with the Wind* was too long.' These remarks tell us all we need to know, ie the length should be fitted to the task; and if it's interesting people will read a lot, whereas if it's boring they'll read none. An even better authority, David Ogilvy (who will read Collister's silly remark and weep), says long copy always works better than short. That may not necessarily be true, though I have found it so, but the only research I've seen, by McGraw-Hill some years ago, found readership of ads in *Business Week* with over a thousand words was about 25 per cent higher than amongst those with less.

Long copy is no indulgence; it is exactly the opposite – bloody hard to write. Nor is literacy irrelevant unless you are writing to illiterates. I admit this is true of most customers and almost everyone who writes marketing or advertising documents, but it is probably less so in the case of those with lots of money. And whilst stupid people's money looks and spends the same as everyone else's, you will probably find your efforts better rewarded among the rich than the poor. Moreover, though we are all (contrary to what some politicians tell you) more prosperous than we were, the rich are, sadly, getting relatively richer and the poor poorer; and if you want to take big money off rich people then long, literate copy is more likely to do it than short, illiterate copy. Is that clear?

NOTE: The blond and amazingly handsome John Hegarty is one of the founders of a very successful advertising agency called Bartle, Bogle, Hegarty, whose name over the years has given much innocent pleasure and aid to comedians short of jokes. Not unlike the town I grew up in: Ashton-under-Lyne.

□ □ □

DATE: DECEMBER 1995

IS IT A BRIGHT IDEA TO TRY TO TEACH CREATIVITY?

Those of you who imagine nought exists 'below the line' save a squalid swamp of bad taste may be surprised to know there is a direct marketing body called the Creative Council – but there is. Recently they produced a fine little newsletter in which their chairman, one Jim Brackin, wrote a tantrum-filled piece under the heading of 'Get It Off Your Chest' – a rather unfortunate title once associated with sundry onanistic activities.

His purpose was to assault 'a bunch of gurus, old lags and wannabees', who claim to sell the secrets of creativity for £250 in two days and who, it seems, make him 'sick'. I quickly checked to see if I was among the guilty parties before deciding he was attacking a seminar featuring scamps like John Watson, chairman of Europe's largest direct marketing agency, George Maves, one of the United States' most able copywriters on finance and insurance, and Chris Barraclough, the not entirely incompetent creative director of an agency bearing his name. Paradoxically enough, even Mr Brackin has been known to stand up and reveal a few of his cherished secrets to paying audiences.

What worried me about his onslaught was that careless readers might conclude courses or seminars on creativity are a waste of time. He was concerned that client or account handlers attend these seminars and, armed with a fistful of laundry lists for success, tend to thrust them on agency people without fully understanding their context. He has a point there. I am often surprised how, after I have pointed out, for instance, that large

> **His purpose was to assault 'a bunch of gurus, old lags and wannabees', who claim to sell the secrets of creativity.**

volumes of type reversed out or in sans serif face or entirely in capitals are very hard to read, eager students have concluded you should use none of them under any circumstance.

But can 'creativity' be taught? Well, I don't suppose you can take somebody as creative as two short planks and magically infuse them with imaginative powers. However, if we assume everyone has **some** scintilla of imagination within them, then surely meeting outstanding exponents, hearing them explain why they do what they do and listening to the principles which guide them can't be a bad thing. If it were, surely almost all teaching would be a waste of time and creative directors themselves unnecessary. (I assume even Jim Brackin tries to guide his people in the paths of virtue.)

For my part I recall seeing on TV master classes on subjects I know **nothing** about – Casals on playing the cello or Wynton Marsalis on jazz composition – which I am sure inspired me to do better, just as, in a more familiar sphere, George Orwell or Somerset Maugham on writing helped me improve, or so I imagine. I find Brackin's case both specious and ill thought-out. For a start, I don't know anybody who purports to 'teach creativity' in either the direct marketing or the advertising industry. But many try to help you do better, and I'm sure it works.

But what worries me is that his views approach perilously close to the 'express yourself' mantra which has left us with an entire generation who can neither write, count, nor draw. Do I sound like an old reactionary? Good!

NOTE: I have talked about this mysterious line that exists in marketing elsewhere. Generally 'above the line' – which means advertising – is seen as a much smarter area to work in than 'below the line' – which means everything else, like direct mail or sales promotion. Advertising people look down on their below-the-line brethren, who envy and sometimes even hate them.

□ □ □

DATE: AUGUST 1995

118

LETTER-PERFECT

Is there one of you who hasn't experienced that infuriating feeling when someone says something insulting to you, you're lost for a reply and then, too late, you think up a devastating one? This is what the French call *'l'esprit de l'escalier'* – the wit of the staircase – something that occurs to you on the way out. In my case, it takes rather longer, maybe because I'm not French.

Not long ago I made the mistake of going into a meeting with a copy of *The Penguin Dictionary of Modern Humorous Quotations*. This gave rise to guffaws all round, implying I had been found out and my occasional literary references come ready-made. I could do little at the time save deny it, merely observing rather feebly that the book in question was not very good, which it isn't. It contains far too many extracts from old BBC radio scripts that have not worn well at all. What I should have

> The true use of a letter is to let one know that one is remembered and valued.

done, as I realized later, was respond in the most wonderfully apposite way: 'It is a good thing for uneducated men to read books of quotations' (Winston Churchill).

In any case, they underestimated me. I own not one such anthology, but quite a few. Their plots lack a certain tension and narrative flow, but I believe the right quotation is like distilled wisdom. The following, on letter writing, could certainly be read to good effect by many who send out direct mail.

A somewhat languid *cri de cœur* on what I assume was early 18th-century junk mail came from Millamant in William Congreve's The *Way Of The World*: 'O ay, letters – I have letters – I am persecuted with letters – I hate letters – no body knows how to write letters; and yet one has 'em, one does not know why – They serve one to pin up one's hair.'

Those who write (or sanction) dull letters should memorize Jane Austen: 'I have now attained the true art of letter-writing, which we are always told is to express on paper exactly what one would say to the same person by word of mouth.' Those whose loyalty programmes recruit with bribes and then fail to communicate might appreciate James Russell Lowell: 'The true use of a letter is to let one know that one is remembered and valued.'

'I like letters to be personal – very personal – and then stop,' said Walt Whitman; and Charles Dickens in *The Pickwick Papers* has a neat exchange between the Wellers: '"That's rayther a sudden pull up, ain't it, Sammy?" inquired Mr Weller. "Not a bit on it," said Sam; "she'll vish there wos more, and that's the great art o' letter writin'."' The classic on length is, of course, Blaise Pascal: 'I have made this letter longer than usual, only because I have not had the time to make it shorter.'

Mail-order writers know the power of the PS – but others did first: 'I knew one, that when he wrote a letter, he would put that which was most material, in the Post-script, as if it had been a by-matter' (Francis Bacon, in his essay *Of Cunning*).

And Sir Richard Steele, in *The Spectator*: 'A woman seldom writes her mind but in her postscript.' Hmm.

NOTE: If one of your jobs is to write letters that persuade others to do what you want, you may find *How to Write a Sales Letter that Sells!* by Drayton Bird (1997) helpful.

□ □ □

DATE: MAY 1997

SMALL TALENT, BIG TEMPERAMENT

I apologize if what follows is wrongly quoted but it certainly isn't misattributed, since I haven't the faintest idea who said it – though you may. It's a rather neat dismissal by a critic of some artistic effort or other. It runs something like 'Those who enjoy that sort of thing will enjoy this very much.'

Anyhow, high on the list of things I enjoy is reading about the early days of today's biggest entertainment industry, pop music – especially when it involves unusually attractive people. This fascination recently led me to the autobiography of the dangerously sexy Ronnie Spector, lead singer of the Ronettes. She and her group were among the inspirations of the Beatles. Even if you're too young to remember the Ronettes, you recall them, don't you?

> **A** young university student asked me a while ago: 'Why are so many advertising creative directors so bloody unpleasant and conceited?'

Describing her first tour in the early 60s Ronnie tells some revealing stories about the temperamental aberrations of some of the big names at that time, one of which stuck in my head because it destroyed for ever my partiality for another artist of the period, Dusty Springfield. Apparently when in pre-concert mode, sooty-eyed Springfield, rather than just chew her nails like any nervous person, used to while away the time by throwing crockery at her dressing-room door. If there weren't enough to hand, as it were, some poor minion had to go to the nearest hardware store and buy more. This naturally made life difficult for other people on the tour, even if compared to the antics of more recent performers like the brothers Gallagher she was a paradigm of old-world courtesy.

Why do people who enjoy big reputations for a brief period become so conceited and behave so insanely? In the music industry it's understandable to some degree. The hype is prodigious, the money astonishing. How, for instance, I wondered, was my daughter's musical partner Tricky affected when he saw himself a few months ago on the cover of a magazine wearing a crown of thorns, illustrating a piece that suggested pop music has more influence on young people today than religion (which it almost certainly has)?

But what I find infinitely more amazing is how people in our far-less-interesting business become the happy, but obnoxious victims of overweening narcissism. Indeed, I was prompted to write this piece by a question a young university student asked me a while ago: 'Why are so many advertising creative directors so bloody unpleasant and conceited?' – and gave me a couple of examples.

It's a bit of a mystery, isn't it? How can one feel pleased with oneself at having mastered the trifling art of filling the gaps between soap operas or the space on the back of the paper we wrap fish and chips in – or used to, before today's hygienic Euro-Paradise?

Could it be that these bladders of conceit have no sense of proportion? And this because their minds are so shallow they lack the intellectual enterprise to look around and see how small the business in which they enjoy a certain fleeting fame really is? As Tallulah Bankhead once observed of a play she didn't like: 'There is less in this than meets the eye.'

□ □ □

DATE: OCTOBER 1996

THE BASICS OF POSTERS IGNORED

Have you seen the striking Ben Sherman shirts' poster? It says 'Separated at birth' and shows two animals – one nice, the other nasty – staring at each other in close-up. One is a soppy-looking bulldog, the other the sort of lumpen thug who sets fire to homeless drunks and starts riots at football matches: a large, and as far as I can see, growing market.

Your poster must work in a split second for those driving past to take it in. The revolving kind change too fast for you to read much anyhow. So you must very quickly make a competitive point that benefits your reader and is easily read from afar. In three words plus a logo, the Ben Sherman poster tells its prospects, who only thrive in gangs, that 'animals like you wear Ben Sherman'. Rather like the late Herr Hitler, it attracts the most bestial elements in society brilliantly.

> **D**o you choose your bank because the manager tells jokes he thinks are funny, but which you don't understand?

Two other good campaigns are for Colgate, which promises you won't have to brush your teeth so often, and Cadbury's Snack – about bridging that gap. In one the word 'afternoon' is split in two, with a brick wall between the 'after' and the 'noon'. But these are rare jewels amidst a swamp of shoddy work, which is too wordy, unclear or the result of creative masturbation. One recent campaign thought playing games with the word 'van' would tilt people towards a particular brand. Fat chance. One poster used a snooker player call Ronnie O'Sulli**van**, another Lee **van** Cleef – with the 'van' missing. A Virgin Direct poster says, 'Watch out. Overhead.' I have no idea what this means, and am disinclined to work it out in seconds, which I imagine would be true of most other people.

Recent Nat West posters had type that was too small. In one a dog had just torn a settee apart. The line said, 'Household insurance, including acts of dog.' I saw it several times before getting the point because, like a lot of their customers, I'm stupid. It probably raised guffaws among 'creatives' in the pub after work, but do you choose your bank because the manager tells jokes he thinks are funny, but which you don't understand? Another ill-considered shambles has 26 words – about 21 too many. From far away you can't see the logo, just 'Who's connecting you to the Internet?' When you get close, the answer is, 'Make sure it's a Cisco-powered network service provider.' This raises another question: 'Why should I?'

Threadneedle's poster doesn't say they get good results for investors as it should, because they do. Instead, it claims 'Threadneedle. Leadership in the changing face of investment' – foolish chest-thumping – above a misleading picture of a man with a little girl and a laptop computer. Do they think they're selling computers? And who will stop a car to read two columns of copy in italics? It's just vague piffle on the changing face of a 48-sheet poster.

Most posters, like most print ads, are junk because people don't understand the medium. Rather a shame if you're footing the bill.

NOTE: The poster should be the distillation of your advertising claim. That's why so few are any good. As a matter of interest, the Colgate poster campaign was discovered to be one of the most effective run that year – and their sales climbed rapidly.

□ □ □

DATE: APRIL 1998

THE FIVE DEADLY SINS

Some years ago, after delivering a speech which I thought excellent in every respect, my complacency was ruptured by a cynical New Zealander, who said: 'Well, since you seem to know just about everything, why can't you guarantee success?' Taking swift refuge in unaccustomed modesty I responded that I don't know everything you should do, merely most of the things you shouldn't.

Just as there are universal truths, there are universal failings, and during my years sitting on an aeroplane for Ogilvy & Mather, I noticed five common sins in creative designed to get replies:

> **A**merican Express enjoyed a 30 per cent uplift in sales a few years ago... largely by making the application easier to fill in.

1. Reluctance to get to the point. We copywriters seem to have the mental equivalent of old motor-car engines, which need to be warmed up for a few minutes. We often put in a couple of paragraphs of waffle before we get to the proposition. Maybe it's fear of being rejected when we do.

2. Being shy about the offer or incentive. Offers harness greed to overcome people's reluctance to read and their reluctance to reply. Unless you have good reason to do otherwise, the offer should be impossible to ignore.

3. Forgetting that there must be something for the reader wherever that reader looks. Hardly surprisingly, bold elements in ads attract most attention and the same applies to mailings. The reader's eye may turn first to the letter, the brochure, the order form or some other piece in the mailing. Make sure your most prominent benefit and your offer are boldly featured wherever that reader may glance.

4. Making it hard to respond. American Express enjoyed a 30 per cent

uplift in sales a few years ago in one highly competitive market, largely by making the application easier to fill in.

5. Failing to do a **complete** selling job. I am not among those who believe the copy should be as long as possible. However, unless you give every sensible reason why somebody should respond and overcome every reasonable objection they may have to doing so, you will not do as well as you could.

Years ago, when working on the *Reader's Digest* record business, I noticed that if we did not list every tune in a compilation ad we lost sales. People look for their favourite tune. If it's not there, they won't buy.

One respect in which people most often fail is in not putting in testimonials or impartial proof that what you say is true. As David Ogilvy once said: 'Why should anyone believe the word of an anonymous copywriter?' My former partner, Brian Thomas, a fount of good sense, once told a school of salesmanship to try putting a testimonial in their mailing. This did so well they put in four more. Sales went up again. They ended up sending out **50** copies of testimonials from satisfied customers.

Simple. Obvious. But then, most of the things that make the big differences in business are simple and obvious.

□ □ □

DATE: JUNE 1993

THE SHEEPISH TENDENCY

My granddaughter Sophie calls me Grandpa Sheep, associating me not with my loving nature but our modest flock of those amiable ruminants in Somerset. In fact some years ago in New Zealand a seminar delegate, hearing me say I kept sheep, asked how many. My reply – '32' – produced hoots of laughter, one wag even asking, 'D'you know 'em all by name then, Drayton?' I said I didn't, but that the chief sheep was called Mrs B.

This fearless quadruped had a super-natural ability to direct her colleagues through the thickest of obstacles to fields not belonging to us. Wherever she went, they obediently followed – which reminds me of fashions in advertising, especially art direction. Someone devises a certain look and everyone copies it without regard for sense or reading habits. For example, a fashion arose in the 60s for kerning the letters in headings so they touched each other. This was done originally to make the type-size bigger in headlines but this was soon forgotten, and practically every headline featured this treatment. Unfortunate, since the effect is to make a headline harder to read.

> I asked the best art director I know... what he thought the greatest sin in art direction. He replied: 'Affectation. Drawing attention to itself.'

A more recent instance is the vogue for the style of typography used on 18th-century tombstones, where some words are italicized or capitalized. The originator of the current trend did it to stress important words, but this was soon forgotten in the Gadarene rush to copy the technique without comprehending the reasons.

A while ago I asked the best art director I know, my old friend and colleague Chris Jones, who has won nearly 100 awards around the world for his work, what he thought the greatest sin in art direction. He replied: 'Affectation. Drawing attention to itself.' One current style does this by scattering sans serif words all over the page, some larger than others, through which the reader must struggle valiantly to extract some sense. This is perhaps done because it will 'involve' the reader. Whoever thinks so is a clot. In western Europe we are accustomed to read from left to right, not up and down or wiggly-waggly, which tires the eye. Obscurity leads not to involvement but exhaustion.

Just as foolish a practice is setting long-body copy in capitals. The eye recognizes shapes, not individual letters. Words set entirely in capitals diminish the shape, whereas the descenders and ascenders in words make those shapes clearer. Once again, the eye quickly tires and the reader gives up. It is also unwise to set large volumes of type in sans serif type without adequate leading. The lack of serif means the eye tends to slip from line to line, making reading difficult.

Are these mere fancies of mine? No: they come entirely from research conducted by Colin Wheildon at the University of New South Wales, who spent two years learning how different layouts and type styles affected comprehension amongst a group of nearly 200 consumers.

The eminent typographer Stanley Morison put the matter as well as anyone could over sixty years ago: 'Any disposition of type... which comes between the reader and the meaning is wrong.' But tell that to the sheep.

NOTE: Colin Wheildon's book *Type and Layout* (1995) is well worth reading, and very amusing in places.

□ □ □

DATE: OCTOBER 1995

YOU DON'T HAVE TO SAY YOU LOVE ME

Whilst mining for gems in old magazines my eye was caught by a piece about Scottish Amicable's head of marketing, Brendan Llewelyn, who has left to start a marketing consultancy. It said he was 'well known for a series of high-profile ad campaigns', which included something to do with 'You've Been Framed' and 'Captain Chaos'.

How that grinning buffoon Jeremy Beadle relates to insurance I cannot surmise. Maybe a policy has been devised to compensate you if by mischance you catch sight of him on television. However as a Scottish Amicable punter I suspected at one point that Captain Chaos was in charge of their customer communications.

> **A** New York beer called Piel's used to run very popular cartoon commercials. Every time they ran, the sales went down.

The piece referred to the Captain Chaos advertising 'era', which I recall more as a fleeting moment. Brendan commented on it with a frankness as refreshing as it is rare among those in his position: 'The idea was to come up with a campaign which was universally likeable, but unfortunately it didn't achieve universal likeability. And because it had such high impact those who didn't like it were very vociferous.'

The managing director of Scottish Amicable said Brendan will 'still have input into our future marketing strategy'. ('Have input into', I assume, means 'advise on'.) I trust he will not suggest more attempts at likeability, which can be quite an overrated commodity. There is a lot of evidence to suggest that my liking you or your advertising may not be enough to make me buy from you. For example, I may love you because you're an amiable half-wit, which, who knows, may have been the case with Captain Chaos.

From what little I recall, that particular creative landmark managed with brilliant simultaneity to communicate all the wrong thoughts about insurance, starting with a strained attempt at humour, whilst employing the one medium which has high attention value but is almost certain to diminish credibility – the cartoon.

Insurance deals with two elements, neither of which is hilarious: nasty possibilities and money. Catastrophe, death, maiming and penury are not funny unless they happen to people you don't like. Nor is finance a rib-tickling matter. Consider the phrase 'laughing all the way to the bank'. I don't know anyone who does. Not those who work in banks, who are worried about being fired, unless they're at head office organizing the firings; and certainly not their customers, who often have similar worries. I find it hard to summon up as much as a wintry smile when I visit mine.

Those thoughts were prompted by another news item I came across in *Advertising Age* a few weeks ago. Budweiser has been running a campaign that is their most popular for years. It came out number one across a wide range of measures including noting, likeability and memorability throughout the first three-quarters of 1995. During the same period sales went down 4.3 per cent.

There is nothing freakish about this. A New York beer called Piel's used to run very popular cartoon commercials. Every time they ran, the sales went down. Every time they took them off, the public complained – so they brought them back. You don't see much Piel's around nowadays.

□ □ □

DATE: APRIL 1996

THE WONDERS
OF TECHNOLOGY

Introduction

As a small boy I was forced to learn carpentry. My innate talents were so tiny that I was daunted and eventually defeated by the challenge of making a wooden tablemat.

I am not sure this task involved what you would call technology, but you must remember that in those far-off days a plane or a pair of pliers was pretty advanced stuff. At any rate, the experience gave me a deep dislike of that sort of thing.

In marketing communications, technology has taken over to an extraordinary degree. This is largely because of the computer, which has developed so fast that a games console now contains more technology than was used in the early space-satellite launches.

I'm never entirely sure of the benefits. The computer lets you send out millions of messages, all personalized, for far less than was ever previously possible. This still leaves room for some amazing mistakes. My favourite was the time a few years ago when American Express, my then client, sent a letter addressed to HM Queen, Buckingham Palace. They got a very polite reply.

A graver problem is that the people you need to write cogent, persuasive marketing messages are in increasingly short supply. Maybe that's because although I was cruelly forced to make tablemats, at the same time I was wisely taught how to read and write – a skill apparently beyond many teachers nowadays.

DANGEROUS OVERSTATEMENTS

I was going to regale you this week with some extreme views about posters, but that will have to await a little historical reconstruction. The reason for this state of affairs will happily confirm the views of those among you who suspect I am not one tenth as smart as I try to appear in these pages.

Last week somebody stole all our computers. As a result my stockpile of prefabricated witticisms has vanished, because neither my PA, the radiant Denise, nor I have had the sense to have a back-up disk. There is some dispute between us as to whether that is her fault or mine. My position is that she knows damn well that I'm an incompetent fool, and should allow for it. I have yet to hear her opinion.

> **J**ohn 'thought his lovemaking days were over when a flesh-eating bug destroyed all the skin on his privates'.

Anyhow, as press date neared, this catastrophe led me to reflect gloomily that I would either have to have some new ideas or start making things up. Happily, on the way back from the airport I found a copy of the *Sun*, whose content confirmed gloriously that truth is stranger than fiction. Who could invent the heart-warming story of 'Superdad John Warman', who has just fathered his 16th child using a surgically created 10-inch Hampton designed by his wife or rather common-law wife, 'beaming Jenny'?

Why was Jenny beaming? It seems the reassembly of said organ was required because John 'thought his lovemaking days were over when a flesh-eating bug destroyed all the skin on his privates'. When asked by the hospital registrar to draw the dong of her dreams, she set to with a will, saying, 'This was too good a chance to miss.' Jobless John is bringing up his kids (fathered on six different women) on £16,000 a year state benefits; and the remarkable operation I have just described was, of course, paid for by you and me.

After that, the *Evening Standard*'s media column was a big letdown. Steve Grime of Leagas Shafron Davis Ayer says, 'Our trade is becoming an easier target for the press than the royal family.' Trevor Beattie of TBWA is even more hurt at the way our skills are disparaged. 'I am a human being. Give me a break. We are not faceless, soulless gits in stripy shirts,' he claims. 'We sold a million bras in a year and 360 Nissan Micras a week.'

That's a lot of bras 'n' cars. Also a lot of rubbish. Too many advertising people – especially those with creative pretensions – fondly imagine advertising **is** marketing. There are one or two other people involved – those who design and make the product, those who distribute and retail, those who determine the pricing – all very often more critical to success. The Nissan and Wonderbra ads are excellent, but such wild assertions do nothing for advertising's case. And, who knows, I rather suspect the same may apply to the stupendous dimensions of Warman's majestic National Health willy.

□ □ □

DATE: JUNE 1995

DON'T CALL US, BECAUSE WE CERTAINLY WON'T CALL YOU

As you know, Charles Dickens wrote his books as magazine serials – rather like soap operas. I'd never compare my work with even the worst of Dickens, but I'm told some of you diligently keep reading, which encourages me to introduce a fresh episode in the 'Andrew Boddington Chronicles'.

My colleague Andrew wished to upgrade his mobile phone and rang his service provider, Astec, hoping his prodigious expenditure entitled him to a reward. Nothing happened until I wrote about it in these pages. Then the chairman of Astec contacted him with admirable speed and said he would sort it out. It seems Andrew was entitled not just to one reward but to so many he was almost embarrassed. Eventually he bought a dinky new phone with many whiz-bang features, and the upheaval of a new number, but before then he went away, telling Astec not to contact him while he was away. In his absence there was a flurry of sales calls.

> **T**he wondrous instrument was sub-contracted to a courier company who despite being given the address said they couldn't find it.

The delivery of the wondrous instrument was sub-contracted to a courier company who despite being given the address said they couldn't find it. Being out the next day, he asked to have it sent to our offices instead. The couriers, using their initiative, went to the first address. As Andrew wasn't there, they gave it to a neighbour – who was not a neighbour but a man decorating the neighbours' house while they were on holiday. So it was locked in their house till they returned.

Astec bent over backwards to rush a replacement to Andrew. The courier even found the right address, and Astec said, no worries, they would arrange collection of the locked-in phone. They never did. Finally the neighbour gave it to Andrew, who commendably didn't sell it to a friend but rang Astec to ask what to do. He was put on to a message box, which promised that the person at the other end would get back to him, which no one did for three days. This happened twice.

It's easy to see how organizations fall apart internally despite their verbal intentions – because to be fair Astec said things would happen, and they did, in a fashion. Either they don't talk to each other, or if they do, messages take too long to get through; and they don't learn from their mistakes. For instance during the early part of this epic Andrew coincidentally received a crass, ill-written letter telling him vaguely of the privileges he was entitled to. Helpfully Andrew took the trouble to critique it to the chairman. He got an identical one three weeks later.

An old Polish curse runs: 'May your dreams come true.' Being digital, the new phone is claimed to work much better. Sadly, it often takes longer to find a free line than the previous one, is prone to even worse reception and cuts off in the same old way. It also seems to have huge blind – or should one say deaf? – spots where he can't use it. More worryingly, these spots are very common in the Home Counties, where it should work best.

What now? Well, the chairman of Astec has said he will make sure Andrew is fully satisfied. Andrew is about to go back and say he isn't. I can't wait to see what happens next.

NOTE: How did this enthralling saga end? Astec carried on in the same slipshod fashion, got bought by Vodafone and probably everyone concerned made a mint. I hesitate to draw any morals from this, except that Andrew switched to Cellnet and has lived happily ever after.

□ □ □

DATE: AUGUST 1995

136

MOBILES, TURTLES AND RUSSIANS

Never mind the wretched Internet: what about the phone? A Henley Centre report by my old colleague Melanie Howard claims some 18.2 million customers were lost last year by retail, travel, banking and leisure firms who don't use it properly. God knows what the US figure is. In California I recently spent an hour getting through to United Airlines, and getting no answer at all from Delta.

And never mind the hazards of the ordinary phone, what about its evil twin, the mobile? Most of my family and colleagues have them, but I have held aloof. It's hard enough to find time to think in these harried times without people disturbing you night and day

> She screamed, 'My eardrums,' and hurled herself at him like an Exocet missile, seizing his head in a vice-like grip.

wherever you are, about things that can usually wait. There's no escaping the bloody machines, though. No matter where I go, their aural pollution seeks me out. The other day for instance whilst quietly solacing myself with a thoughtful pint in 'Cooper's', the Euston Station bar, my reverie was shattered by some braying loudmouth. You know the sort – badly matched shirt and tie, telling the whole world his business, every other sentence ending in a redundant 'right'.

I thought these wretches became extinct in the 80s, but no. He was something ghastly in the City and was boasting about his triumphs in some complicated deal involving a bewildering variety of countries, companies and transactions. I could hardly help laughing aloud when he urged his interlocutor to be careful: 'Of course, this is strictly between you and me, Billy' – and just about everyone in the N1 postal district.

How fortunate for him that he was sitting next to a coward like me, rather than the heroic Amazon I read about recently in the Northern edition of that admirable journal, *The Big Issue*. The piece (by Paul Sussman, whom I applaud) suggested mobiles are not just maddening but downright hazardous. According to him they send out microwaves that cause a number of nasty side-effects, including cancer, whilst an accountant called Stark nearly died a violent – though probably richly deserved – death in Seattle as a result of using one of these instruments of Satan.

He made the mistake of trifling with an 86-year-old, Myrtle Bogosian, whose equanimity he disturbed on the train with his noisiness. She signalled her irritation by clicking her tongue and flaring her nostrils (I would love to have seen that proud equine reaction). When he ignored her, she prodded him with her foot. When this had no effect, she screamed, 'My eardrums,' and hurled herself at him like an Exocet missile, seizing his head in a vice-like grip.

When he tried to free himself, he claimed that she bit his ear. Then he fell on an umbrella. The article does not say whose umbrella it was, but it punctured his lung. Only emergency surgery saved his life. The heroine of this encounter was unapologetic. 'I hate mobile phones, Russians and turtles, in that order,' she stated.

I love people who stand up for their beliefs. But why turtles? Russians, I can understand. But what have those harmless amphibians ever done to compare with the depredations of these beastly phones?

NOTE: You've guessed it. Eventually I got a mobile and started having my own loud, stupid conversations in public places – so many and so rambling, in fact, that my financial director rang me up to cut down on my outrageous bills.

□ □ □

DATE: AUGUST 1996

THE FUTURE IS NEVER AS ADVERTISED

People jump to some bizarre conclusions in this business. I wrote a year ago about a presentation which moved me to giggles, when an otherwise very level-headed lady from O & M Direct implied consumers could have a relationship with a packet of crisps.

I recalled this when reading about a CIA Sensor survey, which revealed that 20 per cent of UK adults would buy a car over the telephone, 26 per cent would buy financial services by direct mail and 49 per cent would buy a PC from a catalogue. So what else is new? Over 10 years ago my agency created a Comp-U-Card mailing which sold two Bentley Turbo motor cars through the post.

> **Most sane people have no desire to have relationships with businesses – for good reasons.**

Anthony Jones of CIA Medialab concluded that the survey proved 'the UK consumer is interested in building a relationship with businesses'. I would humbly suggest it proves nothing of the sort. Most sane people have no desire to have relationships with businesses – for good reasons. To start with they aren't much fun to be with compared to people. I mean, when did you last want to go to bed with a corporation? I would go further: many businesses behave in such a grasping, even dishonourable way nowadays that nobody would have anything to do with them at all if they could possibly avoid it.

Another subject people jump to conclusions about without thinking carefully is the Internet. There are several issues relating to this modern marvel which are little discussed, including the fact that telephone companies are beginning to get pretty pissed off by the fact they are providing a very cheap, and sometimes free, infrastructure that enables too many other people to exploit them. I don't see this lasting for ever. But one point of view that struck a chord with me recently was very well put on 13 June by Walter S Mossberg, technology correspondent of the *Wall Street Journal*.

First, he pointed out that even in the US where the PC has penetrated most deeply only 35–40 per cent of homes have one. Fewer still have a modem that lets them use the Internet. By contrast more than 90 per cent of US homes have mass-market devices like telephones and televisions.

He doubts if the PC as we know it can get much past 50 per cent penetration – too little to make the Internet a real mass medium – and then proceeds to say it is too complicated, too costly and too unreliable, and 'Most non-technical PC owners own nothing that fails to work as frequently. If TV sets or even cars suffered as many glitches, bugs and incompatibilities, as many freeze-ups and crashes as PCs, Congress would be holding hearings.' Amen! Why, for instance, is it so hard to send faxes without problems?

He thinks a new kind of device is needed: an 'info-appliance' that does a few common tasks including browsing the Internet and does them really well without all the hassles associated with the PC. He doesn't know whether this device will come from consumer electronics firms or computer companies, and doesn't care either, as long as someone makes one. IBM apparently is developing something similar: a 'dumb terminal'. Do you think it'll work? The name hardly inspires confidence.

NOTE: The Internet has changed a lot in the three and a half years since I wrote this. I could have been even more wrong than I was – and quite a lot of what I wrote I stand by. In fact people are so keen to get on to the Internet that 'free' providers are making fortunes from the phone companies for either connecting subscribers very slowly, or not at all. It won't last.

□ □ □

DATE: JULY 1996

THE JOYS OF MODERN COMMUNICATIONS

When enthusiasts first explained the Internet and all that jazz to you, what did you expect? I certainly never knew my friends around the world were so eager to shower me with bad jokes. It's a nightmare.

Mind you, I was intrigued by the new Russian pornography service so thoughtfully brought to my attention. How, I wondered, does Russian porn differ from the good old US variety mostly offered? Do they do weird things to each other with borscht? Does each nude model unscrew to unveil a slightly smaller one? Nothing so ingenious. It is what they call in the motor trade 'badge engineering'. Apart from the name 'Russian', the delights that unfold seem identical, right down to the tasteful descriptions.

> **Their Internet sales last Christmas were exceeded only by those of their most successful store on 34th Street in New York.**

I appreciate there is a rich tradition in business whereby nobody ever studies the past because that way we can all squander money, repeating the same mistakes every decade. However this problem of having too much stuff to plough through – direct mail, memos, e-mail – is not new. In the late 14th century, an agent of Signor Datini, an Italian merchant, complained that 'we spend half our time reading letters or answering them'. No great surprise there, because Datini was clearly the partner from hell. Between 1364 and 1410 he exchanged 156,549 letters with his associates. For a number of years he had 10,000 letters zipping back and forth all over southern Europe annually. I learnt that from Worldly Goods by Professor Lisa Jardine (1997), a very entertaining read based on the obvious thesis that in the Renaissance rich people were just as vain, flashy and grasping as they are now.

At the time, it was thought the new invention of printing would make life easier – just as people expect great wonders from the Internet now. Well, in some ways it did, and in others it didn't. Every time a new medium emerges – radio, the cinema, TV – the experts tell you it will render one or more of its predecessors irrelevant. Yet usually nothing of the sort happens. We seem to have an insatiable appetite for messages of all kinds.

The big thing about the Internet to me is that it is a perfect direct marketing medium – especially if you sell to the right sort of people, ie those rich enough to have PCs. The Gap has enjoyed huge success. Their Internet sales last Christmas were exceeded only by those of their most successful store on 34th Street in New York, and now they are starting a separate Internet business.

I am a classic late adopter, but I have finally succumbed to the Internet's charms. My colleagues and I have just spent six months putting together a Web site, www.draytonbird.com, which tells you everything you ever wanted to know – and probably a lot you don't – about direct marketing and related subjects. It's all free, and you can even win a rather predictable prize, but watch out for the usual inept onslaught on your budgets. We do take 'no' for an answer, though – and I'd appreciate your comments.

NOTE: The Web site I was puffing in this piece so shamelessly turned out quite well. For those who understand these things, it is very sticky. Visitors stay for an average of over 23 minutes.

□ □ □

DATE: JUNE 1998

142

THE POWER OF MARKETING GROSSLY OVERESTIMATED

I don't suppose many of you have read one of the silliest books ever written about our business, a 1950s best-seller called *The Hidden Persuaders*. It put the wind up people by suggesting advertising could sell things without them even knowing it.

The idea was that through some magical process slogans – like 'drink Coke' – were being flashed onto the screen so fast that people didn't notice them consciously but were influenced 'subliminally'. I always thought it was complete bunk, like the phoney research about second-hand smoking or recovered memory syndrome. Despite my unjustified opinion of myself, I can't

> The truth was Amex were spending too much on getting poor-quality new customers and not enough on keeping the ones they had.

believe muttering 'Drayton is gorgeous' too fast for people to hear – no matter how passionately – will increase my exiguous fan club.

As you and I know very well, consumers are distressingly unwilling to do as they're told, no matter how many desperate stratagems we try. Far from directing their thoughts, for the most part we are wildly attempting just about anything in the desperate hope that they'll do what we want just occasionally. Nevertheless a strong belief in our mystical powers exists, often among people who should know better.

A few years ago, for instance, when American Express were in the dumps, they thought new advertising would fix things. They switched their account briefly from O & M to Chiat Day, which didn't understand their business and produced some very poor work as a result. The truth was Amex were spending too much on getting poor-quality new customers and not enough on keeping the ones they had (a common vice). What's more, outlets resented their high commission rates. Marketing techniques alone cannot solve such issues; they can only contribute to the solution. When they were addressed, things got better.

Those most gullible about the power of marketing know least about it – privatized firms, for example. Few seem to grasp the simple fact that unless you deliver the goods, all the marketing ploys in the world won't help. Thus, I was sitting on Late Western Railways the other week taking four hours to make a two-hour journey to Somerset. Would belonging to their first-class travellers club, Merlin, have helped? The reverse, I fear – especially as my rage was supercharged by knowing the jumped-up booking clerks in charge had just become millionaires. Though perhaps Merlin membership gives you a wizard-like ability to predict when the train will arrive at your destination.

It's amazing how much money some of these people are making. There was a general howl of outrage when a bloated functionary in one of the utilities, a man called Lewis (presumably a meter reader who oozed his way to the top), was found to have paid himself £3 million last year – a reward, one assumes, for playing his inadequate part in a not very good job of supplying us with gas, electricity or whatever.

Actually it was a bonus for getting away with incompetence without punishment, only possible because of the fiscal ineptitude of the last Government. Another example of the golden rule Blair's crew are revalidating: politicians invariably screw up businesses; and business people usually fail in politics.

NOTE: The Thatcher and Major governments sold off, or privatized, public utilities at knockdown prices. Those who then ran them – mostly the people who had done so when they were nationalized – made disgusting amounts of money extremely fast, rarely by improving service more than utterly necessary.

□ □ □

DATE: APRIL 1998

VIRTUALLY PERFECT

Shakespeare referred to the soldier's 'bubble reputation won in the cannon's mouth'; and if ever there were an industry for bubble reputations it is ours. Transience is always in vogue and tiny achievements loom as large as leviathans.

Of no organization was this truer than of Chiat Day, who became amazingly fashionable, as far as I can make out largely on the basis of one fine, though derivative commercial for Apple, which ran just once, during the 1984 Superbowl. As we all know, Chiat's profits did not match their reputation and they ended up having to sell out to Mammon in the form of True North Communications. Money isn't everything, though, and they always intrigued me, particularly when I read some time ago that they had restructured their agency as a virtual office, especially since I have run my business that way for four years.

> I have had to forgo... my favourite indoor sport:... going round the creative department very early in the morning and writing rude comments on people's work.

My motives were nowhere near as high-flown as theirs, and certainly nothing to do with a lust for high technology – I can't even drive a motor car. No: it just seemed to me a cheaper way of running a business, with benefits both for my clients and myself. And so it seems to have proved. I sit with one and a half helpers in my seedy office, whilst my associates work from their grand estates in the Home Counties, busy scribbling, drawing, thinking up absurd excuses for late work, cajoling our clients and doing bizarre things with databases – just like people in real agencies. After initial doubts even our clients appear to like it.

The chief benefit is a better class of person. By offering this freedom I can afford people who with one exception had all previously been either directors or principals in their own agencies, and no longer wanted to work on the usual basis. But for me the greatest benefit is that we have hardly any meetings, about one every six weeks. So we don't waste time talking about such trivia as sexual harassment, secondary smoking, who should go on the board, or whether so-and-so deserves a bigger office, concentrating rather on vital issues such as where to go to lunch and why my daughter's band just failed to win Mercury's Album of the Year award.

I would love to be able to report to you smugly that this is the best of all possible worlds and anybody who operates otherwise is mad. Sadly, this is not true. For the idea to work, you need highly motivated people who enjoy working on their own without supervision. And personally I have had to forgo one or two of the small pleasures I grew to love in larger agencies – in particular my favourite indoor sport since I became too doddery for more active pursuits: going round the creative department very early in the morning and writing rude comments on people's work. Now I have to settle for sending abusive faxes.

Unfortunately the whole idea falls flat on its face when Denise's Mac breaks down and those prats at Apple take forever to come and fix it. Ah well, I suppose you can't have everything.

NOTE: We got rid of Apple and tried a few other brands. It did not help. See 'The future is never as advertised', also in this chapter.

□ □ □

DATE: OCTOBER 1995

WHAT ABOUT THE POOR BLOODY CUSTOMER?

Introduction

If you want to know what preoccupies marketers, you must conduct a jargon-check. The more jargon, the greater the interest.

Today most firms claim to be 'customer-focused' or 'customer-centric'; they have 'customer care' figuring prominently in their plans; many are inaugurating 'customer relationship management' (CRM) programmes. A positive library of jargon has grown up revolving around the customer.

Unfortunately, jargon obscures rather than encourages what needs to be done – especially when initials creep in. For instance, CRM also stands for 'cause-related marketing'. Certainly all this enthusiasm for the theory doesn't always lead to action, as the following pieces show.

The reason is, I suspect, that the people who run firms' marketing are so amazingly bad at telling the people who deal with customers what their latest wheeze is.

Of course half this book wouldn't exist if readers of *Marketing*, clients and colleagues, especially Andrew Boddington, hadn't told me lots of good stories.

In this respect my PA, Denise Rayner, has done heroic work. I suspect she is mentioned more in this book than anyone except David Ogilvy. Maybe she should be running my agency. Who knows? Maybe she already is.

ARE YOU BEING SERVED?

Last month I went to speak for the Peruvian Marketing Institute in Lima – one of those deals where your hosts plead poverty, so instead of money you get a free trip to see the sights, which in Peru are incomparable. The marketers are pretty smart, too, I was surprised to find.

I flew with Continental, once famed as the United States' lousiest airline but now reborn. They have cleverly copied Virgin's Upper Class, which is half-way between business and first, and their limos to the airport, and have won an award for service from the mysterious J D Powers organization – not just once, but twice in a row.

> **B**usiness theorists believe all firms are in the service business nowadays. As far as I can make out most are actually in the good intentions and bullshit business.

I don't know how Powers compile their ratings, but they would have had a swift rethink if they'd been on the flights I took. One limp-wristed steward between Houston and London managed the impressive feat of not smiling once at a passenger in more than nine hours – though he did weaken fleetingly over Nantucket and shoot a quick twitch of the lips at one of his colleagues.

Changing planes at Houston was fun. Eager to welcome the huddled masses willy-nilly, the US perversely insists you go through immigration even if you're not entering the country. Screwy, or what? Anyhow, it certainly made for a fair old scramble. Add my usual confused state after flying over six hours and no wonder I left a bag full of goodies on the plane from Lima. When I asked the 'customer service' guy at Gatwick for help, he faced the problem with enviable equanimity. 'If it was carry-on baggage, that's your fault.' I wonder if BA trained him in the bad old days before he got his present job.

Business theorists believe all firms are in the service business nowadays. As far as I can make out most are actually in the good intentions and bullshit business. This is typified by the cliché-ridden, high-sounding statements many plaster all over the place – usually at points guaranteed to infuriate those of us who are experiencing the opposite of that promised.

BT is, as you would expect, a leader in this particularly infuriating form of corporate masturbation. A few weeks ago I was waiting to pay a phone bill in their Wimbledon shop. There was no queue, the paying-in desk was unmanned and the staff – who could clearly see me standing there – carefully ignored me, rather like languid waiters in a crowded bar. Facing me I saw the following: 'You'll find we're easy to contact, friendly to deal with. We have set ourselves stringent standards in meeting your requirements.' There followed some more waffle about rapid response and a good connection every time, all of which I had time to write down while waiting to be served.

If you have good intentions in your firm, take my advice: for God's sake, keep quiet about them. Your customers couldn't give a hoot about your internal soul-searching. Let the results come as a delightful surprise to them. I think they used to call it 'managing expectations' – but then you've probably forgotten about that. It was the last management fad but three, if my memory serves me right.

□ □ □

DATE: OCTOBER 1997

BRING ON THE CLOWNS

A few days ago the second annual survey on the competitiveness of countries was issued. Britain had slumped to 17th place – just ahead of Chile. The main reason given was poor infrastructure, particularly in education and transport. I would suggest pathetic management leading to low staff morale plays its part, too.

The problem was crystallized wonderfully when I returned recently from France on the P & O ferry, reaching Portsmouth railway station at 9.30 pm. There were no staff and no announcements on the electronic screens – just a message on a blackboard with a number of droll errors of which the best said the station had been struck by 'lighting'. The whole trip was a wonderful insight into how vigorously the ferry companies are working to combat the challenge of the tunnel and how eagerly the railways are struggling to satisfy their customers before privatization.

> When I went to the P & O office to ask them the times of trains I was greeted with the apathetic response, 'We don't store that information.'

On embarkation there was no information on what to do with my luggage as a foot passenger, until a kindly French customs man told me to put it on a conveyor belt; it would be given back to me on arrival. On the ferry out, Brittany Ferries have a kiosk giving advice about travel and attractions in France. I saw nothing similar from P & O on the way back. Nor did the restaurant quell the continentals' fear that all food in Britain consists of overcooked chips, roast beef and overpriced wine. In fact the only imaginative touch was a man making up little figures out of balloons to the great delight of the children – a bit of added value that I think will do more for future sales than anything else on the ferry.

On disembarking, my luggage was delayed just long enough to ensure I missed the 9:25 train to London; though this was with the aid of the bus company, which stated there were frequent buses – which there weren't –

to the station. When I went to the P & O office to ask them the times of trains I was greeted with the apathetic response, 'We don't store that information' – from an indifferent drab sitting behind a computer screen. An impeccably stupid mixture of jargon and uselessness. The first thing people arriving at Portsmouth without a car probably want to know is how to get to London.

On changing money I encountered something else travellers have grown to recognize: bankers' rapacity – a £2.50 minimum charge as opposed to the flat 1 per cent in Normandy. The two-hour train trip to London quickly refreshed my mind as to what makes Britain so very special – no catering facilities, but much to remind me of what I couldn't buy: crushed beer cans, empty plastic McDonald's cups rolling around and the usual stinking toilets. Every senior railway manager should be compelled to use train toilets, chosen at random, every day for a month.

No wonder – another recent statistic – the British Tourist Industry enjoys less and less of the world's tourist trade. To be honest I don't want any more tourists here, but sheer politeness (another fast-vanishing national trait) requires that at least those who come be transported and greeted adequately. To that end intelligent planning will do much better than clowns with balloons.

NOTE: Since this was written, I have seen no more clowns on P & O. Nor any better service.

□ □ □

DATE: SEPTEMBER 1995

CUSTOMER SERVICE: LESS TALK, MORE ACTION PLEASE

Here's a new law for you. 'The more firms talk about customer service, the worse it gets.' Be honest: have you heard more waffle on any other subject in the last five years? But what actually happens?

My PA Denise wanted to know when Cannock Gates would deliver a gazebo. It took three phone calls. During one someone called Emma said, 'You can't expect us to let all our customers know what's happening. We've got lots of them' – which makes you wonder how long they'll stick around. Also, what the hell's going on *chez* Denise? Gazebo? Next she'll want a sauna in the office.

> **M**arks & Spencer have their problems currently, but does the solution really lie in sending their women's wear catalogue to my colleague David Fulton?

Being eager to explore the frontiers of technology I got On Digital, free. Alas, I couldn't 'activate' it as their 'helpline' was almost constantly engaged for a week. Brilliant invention! Brilliant offer! Brilliant management! I know that because I've just read a sycophantic piece about their fast-talking, inspiring, motivating boss. To adapt Edison's remark, less inspiration and more perspiration might help. Then maybe he could motivate his dazzled minions to get a welcome pack out in less than three weeks.

My other new law states: 'The more data a bank has about you, the less intelligently they will use it.' Thus, Barclaycard sent my partner, Andrew Boddington, his new card – then told him to do their job for them. 'If you have authorized any companies to make charges to your previous account number, please advise them of your new account number straight away.'

Baffled, Andrew rang to see if there were any charges. A helpful customer service person said, 'Over the last six months, you don't seem to have any; but anyhow usually they get redirected automatically.' Huh? I like the word 'usually'. How usually did they have in mind? Frequently usually? Occasionally usually? Search me, guv.

Here's another mystery. How did Lloyds become the most successful of the big banks? Was it with pretty new signs? After trying unsuccessfully all morning to talk to my 'personal banker', Denise had to settle for this novel explanation from someone else: 'We have a skeleton staff and we can't always answer the phone. We have to deal with personal customers.' How about a brilliant new invention called the answerphone to apologize, take your number and promise to call back? No wonder the invading US banks are eating these bozos' lunch – as I long ago predicted.

Marks & Spencer have their problems currently, but does the solution really lie in sending their women's wear catalogue to my colleague David Fulton – and not a word about 'the women in your life'? True, David has his mad moments, but he rarely wears women's clothes, however fashionable.

How will Britain's top managers sort out this mess? Why, they'll fire people – lots of them, in fact anybody except those responsible: themselves. The man from the Pru thinks there should be fewer men at the Pru. Abbey National feel they should have fewer counters, and charge so much the customer problem will go away – literally.

The Henley Centre recently revealed that 70 per cent of customers who lapse think they're not getting products, service or communications they want. I may be a stupid old sod, but is degrading all three the answer?

NOTE: As this was published, Stephen Grabiner, the boss of On Digital, resigned to go to a new job, which he did not in fact take, having had a yet better offer elsewhere. Meanwhile a number of financial firms were busy trying to slim down, ie employ fewer people and reduce service.

□ □ □

DATE: JULY 1999

DERRIÈRES TO THE CUSTOMER AT DIXON'S

How hard can it be to buy a pager? Bloody near impossible as far as I can see if you're dealing with Dixon's and you want to do anything that interferes with their droll management processes.

Recently one of my dedicated acolytes decided he couldn't live without one of these ingenious little devices. Since I was brought up when sophisticated communication meant the adroit use of forked twigs to carry messages, I couldn't understand why. But I certainly understood what happened after I decided to humour him and buy the thing.

He went into his local Dixon's branch and asked if they would let us buy a £79.99 pager on our American Express card, and let him collect it. The answer was 'yes'. My office then called up to arrange this complex transaction with the assistant store manager, who kindly took the details of the card and the name of the person.

> It reminded me of something said by 'Neutron Jack' Welch... In bad firms he says people point 'their faces to the chairman and their asses to the customer'.

A little later, after we had gone to this trouble, he called back to say actually we couldn't pay on a card billed to my office and have the wretched thing picked up – even with my written authority. Helpfully, though, he said there was a way to solve the problem: we could fax a company purchase order. We duly did so. Then, at 5.05 in the afternoon the poor fellow called back apologetically. Their head office would not authorize the sale without a letter from our 'holding company'.

You can picture our surprise. We were trying – desperately – to buy something for a measly £79.99. Dixon's were trying – even more desperately – to stop us. The assistant manager could only say, 'It's not my fault – it's head office,' and leave it at that. He was not, in the jargon, 'empowered'.

All this happened on Friday, so we could do nothing more. It was solved over the weekend, when the person concerned went into a small local shop. He found a pager with almost exactly the same features, in fact in some ways better. It was only £59.99. He was asked all the same questions and assured there would be no problem buying it on our charge card. On Tuesday morning we did the deal in five minutes, and my chap was the ecstatic owner of his pager. It took no time at all and saved £20.

I don't mind being ripped off or even screwed around a bit – but Dixon's managed the double. It reminded me of something said by 'Neutron Jack' Welch, one of the great business heroes of our time. He got his nickname from the bomb that kills all the people but leaves the buildings intact, which is more or less what he did when he started running General Electric. He fired just about everybody in sight, taking the firm out of the doldrums to unparalleled success. He clearly understands the difference between well-run firms and disasters. In bad firms he says people point 'their faces to the chairman and their asses to the customer'.

Asses, of course, are not donkeys but the American for arses. Either way they sound remarkably like Dixon's to me.

NOTE: In 'The customer is always wrong, it seems' later in this chapter, you can read how someone important at Dixon's reacted to this – and managed to reinforce the point I was making.

□ □ □

DATE: MAY 1998

NO ROOM – BUT HIGH PRICES – AT THE INN

One of the ladies trusting enough to marry me and masochistic enough to persist sought comfort in a course on antiques restoration before seeking greater solace with a Swedish lawyer.

The course didn't help, as my appearance testifies, but I learnt something valuable. Very often you don't get what you expect when buying an antique. So you won't be amazed to learn that the same might apply to a hotel run by an antique dealer. You don't get what you expect even if you pay through the nose for it.

I found this out recently when I made the dreadful mistake of booking my Australian confrère Malcolm Auld in

> **Many of us in marketing may imagine the lesson of the last 20 years is learnt: that people do understand they must deliver service. Frankly, I fear there has been no change of heart.**

Miller's Hotel, off Westbourne Grove. If you've read this column for a while, you'll know he furnishes me with a regular supply of antipodean jests and anecdotes. Over the years he has helped me cover a number of Aussie esoterica, from the perils of being 'swooped by a maggie' to the depressing ability of otherwise unemployable Poms to get good jobs with trusting firms over there.

The principal thing to be said in Miller's favour is that they've given me some good material in return. 'Miller' is, I understand, the name behind Miller's Antiques Guide. I put Malcolm there because it's near my office, though at £110 a night for a single room in a rather ugly building above a Brazilian restaurant, it's not cheap. As some sort of compensation, though, it is stuffed with fine antiques.

What it is not stuffed with is fine service – or any service worth the name as far as I can discern. If you ring a guest up early (in my case 7.30) in the morning, you get an answerphone. It seems amazing, but from what Malcolm experienced, there's nobody there to look after the guests at night. Is that illegal? It certainly seems dangerous. What happens if all the guests are mired in drunken slumber and a fire breaks out?

On Malcolm's first night, one of his fellow guests experienced Cool Britannia in action. He locked himself out of his room by accident and had to sleep on a couch, warmed by other guests' coats. The next night at midnight Malcolm himself couldn't open the front door and had to go to another hotel. Miller's seemed to doubt his word on this, and when we last spoke he was arguing about whether he should pay for that night.

Many of us in marketing may imagine the lesson of the last 20 years is learnt: that people do understand they must deliver service. Frankly, I fear there has been no change of heart. Many merchants will still rip you off given half the chance – and prosper doing so. The other day a tipster was recommending firms like Connex and Stagecoach as an investment – the very people who make rail travel a misery every day.

The antiques business shows what effrontery and guile can do with a piece of junk. I wonder if Mr Miller's Guide is any more reliable than his hotel.

NOTE: It's amazing how quickly one forgets things in the news. When I wrote this, Mr Blair and his minions were talking about 'repositioning' Britain because the traditional associations – pageantry, the Royal Family and so forth – were not 'cool' enough. Besides being fatuous, this illustrates how people who don't understand marketing properly think it can achieve the impossible. You can't wave a magic wand and change views that have taken centuries to solidify.

□ □ □

DATE: MAY 1998

OPPORTUNITY OR PROBLEM?

A man has just arrived in a new town. He stops someone and asks: 'What are the people here like?' The reply came: 'I think you'll find the people here are pretty much the same as they were where you came from.' I like this story because it illustrates the fact that our attitude is often the most important ingredient in success. The best story I know about that is one you may have heard. But it's worth repeating in case you haven't.

The Czech shoe magnate, Bata, sent a salesman to Africa to check out the prospects. When he arrived the man sent a telegram: 'Nobody here wears shoes. Am coming home.' Bata did not get to run the world's biggest shoe business by accident, but by persistence, which as we all know is a far more essential ingredient than intelligence, imagination or wit. He sent another salesman out who immediately telegrammed back: 'Great opportunity. Nobody here wears shoes.'

> I admire this couple more than many of the high-powered people I meet in marketing. They have the common sense to do the obvious.

This came to mind when I was walking through my local village in my role as general busybody and sensation seeker. Well, something interesting is going on in what business journals call 'the retail environment'. We once had three general stores. One, a mini-market, has always thrived. Another closed down because the people gave up: I suspect they bought it as a retirement hobby, just as people dream of retiring to run a pub. They had not considered another useful ingredient if you want to succeed: knowledge of the subject, in this case retailing. In much the same way few of the many thousands who dream of running a pub bother to learn it's one of the most taxing jobs imaginable, almost sure to ruin your marriage, make you an alcoholic or both.

One of the other stores has always struggled. It used to be called 'The Village Stores'. Then came the first resort of the witless: it was 'rebranded' as

'Cannington Capers'. This failed. A successful publican bought it, but had no luck – probably too busy doing what he does best to learn about running stores. Finally a new couple, Mr and Mrs Stephenson, have turned the place round. Guess what? They had the novel idea of improving the product and the service. They re-laid out the shop – which was quite spacious – to sell more than groceries. Now they run a little café in part of the space and sell videos. They open 7 days a week, 13 hours a day.

I was highly impressed, and asked Mr Stephenson what retailing experience he had. 'None,' he replied. 'I've spent most of my life as a draughtsman.' My God, this couple would have made millions with Kingfisher or someone like that. I asked him their secret. Clearly, it was attitude. 'It's a great opportunity,' he said. 'The agricultural college here is full of kids who like a drink and so on, so we started by offering the things they like, and it worked.'

I admire this couple more than many of the high-powered people I meet in marketing. They have the common sense to do the obvious. All they need now is a mission statement to screw everything up.

□ □ □

DATE: NOVEMBER 1998

SERVICE WITH A SNARL

'Kindly convey my insults to the chef,' I asked the waiter. I didn't really, but I felt like it, because as far as I could see the restaurant – the Rainforest Café near Piccadilly – could do almost everything except cook well.

I was so impressed when I entered that I wondered why they weren't packed out. It's an extraordinary confection of special effects, featuring a hard-working cast of stuffed alligators, chimpanzees, gorillas, baboons, crocodiles, elephants, parrots and who knows what else. My first letdown came when I waited for several minutes in a queue of six people to be seated by the 'greeter' although the place was quite empty. Another was the prices, which clearly had to fund the special effects, but were colossal even so. The food was the final turn-off. If you run a restaurant, no matter how stunning the ambience and willing the service – which indeed it was – it's no bloody use if the food's indifferent and overpriced.

> Who pays for all this? Obviously, we customers. But I feel sorry for the staff, constantly having to deal with and apologize for the incompetence of the management – who should pay for it.

My views were formed early, since my parents' pub–restaurant was in the *Good Food Guide* from its very first issue. One reason was that when some people arrived at 3 am once my mother got up and made them a meal. Now that is service. It happened all of 47 years ago but the message has yet to reach the Legh Arms in frightfully smart Prestbury on the other side of Manchester. They seem to have reversed Unipart's wonderful old slogan, and operate along the lines of 'The answer is no. Now, what's the question?' I had booked for a party of some 20 people. But could we bring in a bottle of champagne if we paid corkage? No, it was 'illegal'! Could I buy a bottle of wine at the bar? Only from the wine waiter. (He was busy.) Could I extract so much as an apology when the waiter spilt gravy on my newly cleaned suit?

Not a ghost of a chance.

Returning to London on Virgin Trains it started again. Could I get a mineral water? No – sold out. Could I get any crisps? No – sold out. Haven't they run this line long enough to notice the last train from Manchester to London on Sunday evenings is crowded, especially on Mother's Day? I never thought I'd end up pining for the return of British Rail.

Who pays for all this? Obviously, we customers. But I feel sorry for the staff, constantly having to deal with and apologize for the incompetence of the management – who **should** pay for it. They're either recruiting the wrong people, or not training them, or not motivating them to do a good job. If the economy is roaring ahead you can get away with this crap but when the downturn comes – what goes up must come down – God knows what will happen. People won't have the money or desire to be insulted in Prestbury; they'll find better ways to get from Manchester to London; and they won't accept special effects as a substitute for decent meals.

☐ ☐ ☐

DATE: APRIL 1998

SERVICE WITH NO LAUGHS

Service is a hobby-horse I mounted some time ago; I do not propose to dismount any time soon, and I hope you endorse this.

Compare two firms and how they treat their customers. The first is engaged in the marketing of the future: they sell a flower delivery service over the Internet. A colleague in Spain tried them out and was delighted to get a message: 'Thank you! You are our first customer in Spain. Please accept $65 worth of flowers, free, to be sent to anybody anywhere in the world.' To adapt the McKinsey motto, they are giving the customer 'a service better than he has any right to expect', perhaps because they are trying hard in a new market.

The second company dominates an old, even dying market. Here's what befell my PA, the lovely Denise, when dealing with Thomson Travel. Denise booked a three-bedded room for herself, husband and four-year-old son, for whom she paid 80 per cent(!) of the adult price. A three-bedded room with cot space was confirmed. What she got was a cramped twin-bedded room with a camp-bed blocking access to the patio doors.

Every reply she has had from him has repeated the words, 'Please bear with us. We will come back to you in due course.'

She complained, only to receive an (unsigned) letter pointing out the small print said some three-bedded rooms have camp-beds. Irrelevant, surely, in view of the confirmed booking. She then wrote to the managing director who passed the buck to his ironically titled 'customer services manager'. She was offered £75 in travel vouchers as compensation. Understandably Denise didn't want a titchy discount on something she had no wish to undergo again.

When she wrote again the customer services manager in turn passed the buck to the travel agent suggesting they misrepresented or misunderstood the facts. The agent, who has been in business (and with whom we have dealt) for many years, was so surprised she checked the 'Hotel Fact Finder'. This clearly states, 'Rooms with 2 single beds plus an extra bed. Some rooms are large enough to take 3 beds plus a cot' – just what Denise expected and did not get.

Still unhappy but commendably optimistic and persistent (how d'you think she puts up with me?) she wrote back to the managing director. He replied, reaffirming his distress at her dissatisfaction and passing the matter back to the customer services manager. Every reply she has had from him has repeated the words, 'Please bear with us. We will come back to you in due course.'

I suspect she'll get a helpful response on the twelfth of never. Have Thomson ever wondered how much better they would do by satisfying complainants, rather than sinuously wriggling to avoid doing so? Research shows how vigorously unhappy customers spread the word, and that satisfied complainants are better customers than if they'd never complained at all. 'If Thomson do it, do it; if they don't, don't' was their old slogan. I can see why they changed it. It was a slip-up by the copywriter. The sense should clearly be the other way round.

Adapt or die is a fine phrase. Mortality rates in the travel business have always been high. On this evidence, the more the merrier.

NOTE: So what happened? Eventually, Denise got a £75 cheque, which did not encourage her to use Thomson again. And Thomson are now in trouble.

□   □   □

DATE: AUGUST 1995

164

Dulux 90BB 22/247

LILAC HEATHER 1

Dulux 90BB 38/186

LILAC HEATHER 2

Dulux 90BB 53/129

LILAC HEATHER 3

Dulux 90BB 68/089

LILAC HEATHER 4

Dulux 90BB 74/038

LILAC HEATHER 5

Dulux 90BB 83/020

FV2

LILAC HEATHER 6

Dulux offers the widest choice of paint colours in a great range of finishes for professionals and consumers. Ask an assistant to mix your colours in store.

All of the colours on this stripe card are available in the following products and finishes...

For Walls & Ceilings

Flat Matt Ultra-matt finish.
Matt Matt finish.
Soft Sheen Mid-sheen finish.
Silk High-sheen finish.

Paints with added extras

All of our colours are also available in a range of paints which are tougher than our standard paints. Perfect for kitchens, bathrooms and anywhere you need added durability.

Ask an assistant in store for more details.

For Wood & Metal

Eggshell Low-sheen contemporary finish.
Satinwood Subtle sheen finish.
Gloss High-sheen finish.

... and remember to try these colours at home first. Just ask an assistant to mix a tester pot in store.

For more technical advice:

Retail Advice Centre Number: **08444 817 817**
or **www.dulux.co.uk**

Trade Advice Centre Number: **08444 817 818**
or e-mail **duluxtrade_advice@ici.com**   03/12

MIX
Paper
FSC   FSC® C102384

THE CUSTOMER IS ALWAYS WRONG, IT SEEMS

Readers often ask how I keep up this tide of bilge, week after punishing week. Whence come the ideas? A cartoon of a critic gloomily seeking inspiration suggests one answer. 'I can't find anything to get angry about' was the caption. So anything stupid gives rise to a good old rant. Another comes when someone contradicts me, giving rise to a good old literary punch-up.

Double thanks, then, to Andrew Owens, Dixon's Financial Operations Director. On 21 May I told how we couldn't buy a cheap pager over the phone from Dixon's with our corporate American Express card, even though one of their shopkeepers assured us

> In short, they bore in mind the words of the immortal David Ogilvy, 'The consumer is not a moron, she is your wife.'

twice that we could. I suggested they cared less about their customers than their systems and that the poor fellow was not allowed to use his own judgement in a small matter.

Mr Owens responded in this journal using the silly politician's trick of ignoring the main point, and gave some statistics on credit-card fraud instead. Forget that another small shop completed the very transaction Dixon's couldn't: how can people all over the world, every day, 24 hours a day ring and buy things with their credit cards? Maybe this breakthrough, which after all is only about 20 years old, has escaped Dixon's notice. In short, Mr Owens made my point for me. I, the customer, was wrong – and their systems were right. But if all we did was complain, what a gloomy world this would be. Compare Dixon's with Colgate-Palmolive.

If you study this column you may notice me refer occasionally to my PA, the fragrant Denise. Why so fragrant, you may ask? Well, she just adores all types of unguents, fragrances, scents, perfumes – indeed anything to make our office ambience agreeable – but she had some trouble with Soft & Gentle Light, an aerosol for intimate usage. So she complained. Here's what Colgate did.

First, they wrote and said sorry. They said that they'd examined the product and there didn't seem anything wrong, but perhaps Denise had some 'idiosyncratic' – and God, is she idiosyncratic – reaction to one of the ingredients. She may have sprayed it too close to where it was supposed to go, a part of the body I hesitate to mention in these genteel pages. They assured her they took great trouble with their products. They made helpful suggestions, explained why sometimes an ingredient can cause problems and ended by apologizing again. In short, they bore in mind the words of the immortal David Ogilvy, 'The consumer is not a moron, she is your wife', or in this case, PA.

What really made Denise happy – I have detected a certain acquisitiveness in her – was that when acknowledging her letter they sent £3 worth of vouchers – then a further £6 worth with their detailed explanation. All this for something costing around a pound.

How did Mr Owens reach his present lofty title without learning that when you mess customers about it's smart to say sorry before you make your threadbare excuses? Maybe because, as I suggested, customers come second with him.

NOTE: It is always worth bearing in mind that research suggests a customer whose complaint is satisfied will become a better customer than if there had never been a problem in the first place. I have mentioned this elsewhere, and sometimes I wonder: could this lead to an interesting strategy for firms that make bad products?

☐ ☐ ☐

DATE: JUNE 1998

THINK A LITTLE –
IT USUALLY PAYS

If you went into an IBM office 20 years ago there was every chance you would see on the wall a plaque bearing the company motto: 'Think.' At some point IBM forgot this admirable injunction and got into a fearful mess. They seem to be climbing out again, so perhaps the signs have reappeared; but why on earth do so few marketers think beyond the obvious?

Take Books Etc. They cheered me up no end about a year ago by advertising that if you didn't like a book you bought there, they'd give you your money back without question. How obliging – and smart, I thought. I devour books by the yard, since I find lots of ideas to steal, and I transferred most of my business to their Queensway branch.

> **T**he whole thing was an impeccable exercise in pissing off a happy customer who with a little thought could have become a friend for life.

When my daughter, bless her, recently bought me *Wild Swans*, which I had already read, I agreed with my strategic adviser, Denise, that they were the people to see. I entered with sprightly step, looking forward to exchanging that book and buying a couple more. The girl at the cash-desk said pleasantly but apologetically, 'They're getting a bit tight on that sort of thing' and hailed a smug young twerp – the manager, I fear – who said 'Sorry' with what seemed uncannily like relish. He couldn't help because it was against their policy: the book was bought in Manchester, where they had no branches. I said, 'Well, I am quite a good customer of yours.' This rang no bells. Maybe his superiors have failed to explain the fairly significant bearing happy customers have on his salary being paid. He was, in the good old-fashioned way, only following orders. I bade him a waspish adieu:

'Congratulations, you've just lost a customer.'

Does their policy make any sense to you? It doesn't to me. Maybe it's to do with stock management. But a best-seller like *Wild Swans* isn't hard to unload. The whole thing was an impeccable exercise in pissing off a happy customer who with a little thought could have become a friend for life – perhaps the chief aim of marketing.

As we all know, research shows happy customers tell fewer people – I've seen figures ranging from three to five – than unhappy ones, who tell between eight and twelve. Clearly people enjoy moaning more than they do being satisfied; but what Books Etc lack, apart from common sense, is an understanding that customers are more important than transactions. A happy customer will generally stay with you for years. I spend about £500 a year on books. So by not doing a favour that would have cost them nothing these people lost revenue over five years of up to £2,500.

Eventually Denise went to Waterstone's, who obliged – and got an order for another, more expensive book, plus a happy customer. Perhaps their people have been given the excellent instruction the staff receive at the best retailers I know, Nordstrom in California: 'Use your best judgement at all times.' Maybe Books Etc think judgement is too important to be left to staff. I often think the same applies with greater force to management and managers.

□ □ □

DATE: FEBRUARY 1996

WATCH OUT, SOPHISTICATES ABOUT

'Find out what people want and need, and give it to them – and you'll get rich,' said an old-time US millionaire. This pithy definition of marketing sprang to mind – not for the first time – after I was savaged by someone from MasterCard a while ago for saying rude things about his barrage balloons.

Dismissively he pointed out that today's financial marketing is far too sophisticated for my poor mind to grasp. Having worked with American Express for 18 years, I doubt that. Their marketing has been infinitely more effective than that of MasterCard, and even someone as stupid as me is bound to pick up a few of the rudiments over such a long period.

> It's no use, for instance, producing multimillion pound commercials with oodles of special effects if you can't communicate properly with your customers.

The problem with financial marketing is not lack of sophistication but a pathetic failure to get simple things right. It's no use, for instance, producing multimillion pound commercials with oodles of special effects if you can't communicate properly with your customers. By that I mean send out letters that are polite, easily understood and easy to reply to.

Take how my colleague Andrew Boddington, who has salted away some of his massive earnings in a savings plan, was treated. Skandia Life sent him a letter reading: 'You have been advised [which he hadn't] by Barclays Bank plc the former assignees, that they no longer have an interest in the above plan. The benefits under the plan have therefore reverted to the policy holder(s)', followed by an illegible signature.

A while later, Barclays did send him a letter, which said: 'We enclose the undermentioned documents. Please sign and return the attached form of receipt', followed by some scrawled numbers and a signature, all virtually indecipherable. Andrew asked himself the sort of questions people who deal with these sophisticated marketers ask all the time. 'Who signed the letters? Do they wish to remain secret? Whom do I ask for if I call? Do these people care at all about me? What exactly are these letters about? Why can't I read the signature in either of them?'

He expressed it simply. 'I put £150 a month into this plan and this is the quality of attention I get. Why can't they just give me the respect due to a customer?' What he should have got was letters from both firms reminding him what the plan involved, refreshing his mind about its present and eventual worth, and telling him what to do. The letters should have noted whom to talk to if he had any questions, and included a free phone number and a reply-paid envelope so it would not cost him money to do these sloths' jobs for them. What hardly any of these people do is pay attention to the detail that alone ensures satisfied customers and without which they will always be at the mercy of anybody who comes along and does the job properly.

This sort of thing is not the exception. It is the rule, and will be as long as conceited (but oh-so-sophisticated) senior marketing people in these institutions fail to ask themselves the simple question: if I were the customer, what would I want? That will do far more good than any amount of jargon about brand values, quality relationships, customer care and the like, which trips so easily off the tongue as the sophisticate's substitute for hard work.

NOTE: Nothing in MasterCard's marketing since I wrote this has suggested they know what they're doing. Visa, who are their main rivals, continue to outperform them easily. And of course financial marketers generally continue to do a dismally bad job.

□ □ □

DATE: NOVEMBER 1996

WHAT ARE THEY DOING WITH YOUR MONEY?

Introduction

In this part of the book we talk about money: marketers who buy and sell money, and how marketers in general waste their money. In both areas, as you will see, some pretty odd things go on. This is a shame, because money wasted on marketing would otherwise end up in your pockets – either as a customer, a shareholder or an employee.

Many marketers seem amazingly reluctant to attempt, even in the vaguest way, to keep tabs on their money. In view of some of the other things you can read in these pages, this may not surprise you. But what is surprising is that when it comes to marketing, banks and other financial institutions, which you would have thought had great respect for money, throw it around like drunken sailors.

Good marketing is actually a service, yet like a lot of so-called service industries, the banking and associated industries find the concept of service strange, if not repugnant. It took them many years indeed to adjust their thinking to the point where they thought they ought to be open when it suited their customers rather than themselves.

I sometimes think that it is going to take quite a few more before they grasp the basics of marketing, particularly advertising. Partly, this is because they took an enormous wrong turn back in the 70s.

Looking around to see who knew most about marketing, and believing that they ought to try it themselves, they saw that the real experts were people like Procter & Gamble and Unilever, who sell soap powder and such. They then hired a few of these people who quite predictably tried to sell financial services in the same way that they sold soap.

It didn't work, and it won't work – but they keep trying.

A FEW WORDS TO THE WISE FROM DENISE

If you were to look through three months' issues of *Marketing*, one thing would undoubtedly strike you: the speed with which people in senior marketing jobs hop from twig to twig. It's a wonder they ever get anything done (and of course many don't).

But another thing would strike you perhaps even more and that is the even greater speed with which senior people on the financial side of marketing change jobs. I can think of quite a number of firms where this applies, though NatWest and the Prudential seem especially flagrant examples.

> **I haven't even had a bloody key-ring from my mortgage provider. At least the people at Safeway or Tesco make some attempt to provide some decent service.**

Why do I say 'flagrant'? To answer that, we must ask why firms are constantly changing these people. Surely this has to be that they don't know what they want from them to start with. Most top managers probably can't even define 'marketing'. As a result they don't know what it is supposed to achieve. And they certainly don't think deeply enough about how well they perform compared to others – not just in their own industry, but outside. In other words, too many are incompetent drones.

All this was put into perspective for me by my PA, the wonderfully down-to-earth Denise, the other day. She was talking about how she gets treated at her supermarket (and she has been known to complain from time to time about this), compared to the treatment she receives from the people who provide her with financial services.

So I thought it a good idea to get her to tell you what she thinks in her own words. After all, the evidence suggests many of you may be too busy writing reports, planning strategies and sorting out your next jobs to spare the time to talk to consumers.

'Let's face it,' she started. 'I haven't even had a bloody key-ring from my mortgage provider. At least the people at Safeway or Tesco make some attempt to provide some decent service.' And having begun, it was hard to stop her (as you will soon discover if you get her on the phone).

'If you think about it: your mortgage provider is getting in the region of £500 a month from you, and all they ever do is increase mortgage rates, tell you how marvellous they are in silly commercials – but never communicate on ways to save you money. For an average £70,000 mortgage you are paying these people in the region of £120,000 – not a bad return for the mortgage provider – and all they do is take the money with absolutely no service except what suits them.

'And compare this with Tesco and the like who offer points as reward for shopping there. Now not many of us are fooled into thinking they are doing this out of the goodness of their hearts, but at least they **are** doing it and attempting to keep your custom. I get something like £20 of vouchers every quarter from Tesco to spend as I like – not a fortune but a good return on an average £40–£50 spend a week on groceries.'

Right on, Denise!

□ □ □

DATE: OCTOBER 1998

A GOOD IDEA OBSCURED BY WAFFLE

Have you ever had the feeling you're being overtaken by events? I felt practically run over two weeks ago. Barely had I sent off my piece asking why Eurostar didn't persist with destination advertising than they stuck up posters everywhere doing just that – very well.

But it is a pleasure to be more or less right from time to time. For years I have suggested to anyone who cared to listen – and quite a few who didn't – that £1 spent communicating with your staff is worth £10 spent against the trade or other intermediaries and £100 spent talking to your ultimate customers.

> **'44** per cent of marketing directors make little effort to share their marketing plans with their own departments and 68 per cent fail to share them with their managerial colleagues.'

This is, of course, a wildly imaginary set of statistics, but I was vastly heartened to read what follows. 'Business leaders who invest in workplace marketing with passion and persistence are found over two years to deliver 77 per cent better return on capital than their competitors, 172 per cent improvement in pre-tax profits and 78 per cent more profit per employee.' (I wonder how those without passion and persistence do, incidentally; and how do you define those rare qualities?)

Also, '44 per cent of marketing directors make little effort to share their marketing plans with their own departments and 68 per cent fail to share them with their managerial colleagues'. And 'less than 10 per cent of companies with "customers", "quality", "service" and/or "people" written into their mission statements can claim a motivated workforce'. (Mind you, I have long suspected any firm with any mission statement is badly run.)

These statistics come from Strategic Management Resources, who help you motivate your staff, which is what they mean by 'workplace marketing'. The former head of the Brann agency runs it, and I think she's on to a good thing. She certainly did a good job at Brann. My only worry is that if people communicate with their employees using as much pretentious jargon as some of the stuff she sent me, they'll just stand around in befuddled confusion.

In their otherwise excellent newsletter, a licensee called Dr Shirley Probert produced a whole page of 100 per cent proof business-school gobbledegook. I have developed a macabre interest in this sort of guff, and even a kind of perverse admiration for its practitioners. How many people can use the phrase 'distinctive competence' four times in three paragraphs, or 'integrate' and 'integrating' three times in one? I was disappointed to spot only one 'holistically'. Dr Probert should try harder.

I believe I may have hesitantly pointed out before on these pages that in this country if you want to write to anyone except business-school denizens, management consultants and such miscreants, the use of relatively comprehensible language is mandatory.

This reminds me of what a famously insensitive 18th-century Scottish judge said when sentencing some poor soul. 'You're a braw wee fellow, but ye'll be nae the worse for being hangit.' Workplace marketing is an excellent idea, but will be none the worse for being explained in English. It shouldn't need to shelter behind obfuscatory drivel.

Mind you, my faithful aide Denise rightly says any communication is better than none and, rather cynically, 'The Americans usually fall for that sort of thing.' What worries me is that more and more of the British do, too.

□ □ □

DATE: MARCH 1998

BEING PROFESSIONAL –
BUT NOT VERY

The big professional firms have suddenly discovered advertising. Not how to do it – most appear to think it is the same thing as boasting – but that it is a good thing.

Andersen Consulting recently announced that they plan to spend $100 million on a world-wide marketing campaign. They ran a campaign last year featuring fish, which I was very rude about. It must have worked, though, because now they have a commercial featuring some planets pulling the moon across the sky – a triumph of special effects over content. One US commentator said, 'I don't think a manager who sees the ad is going to say, "I want to go out and hire these guys", but it differentiates them from the competition.'

> **T**heir slogan is a waste of space and a lie. You'd have to have checked your brain in at the door to believe they focus only on clients.

Of course, the point is that any advertising is better than no advertising – unless it is so bad it puts people off your product or service, which happens less rarely than you might imagine.

By contrast to the multimillion-dollar Andersen effort, an ad in September's *Business Age* has the headline, 'Whose guide to MBOs is priceless, and free?' and beneath it, 'The answer is Deloitte & Touche', and then the slogan, 'focusing only on clients'. It won't get people to hire them, but getting a response is the right first step. Actually, it is the first ad I have seen in this field to boldly offer a useful incentive and go all out for replies – and it would get more if the copy were longer and told you more about the booklet.

Their slogan is a waste of space and a lie. You'd have to have checked your brain in at the door to believe they focus only on clients. Being accountants they focus on their profits just as much, and probably more. However, we must not quibble, because amongst the advertising rules Claude Hopkins laid down 78 years ago in *Scientific Advertising* was 'Offer service' – and that booklet is a genuine service.

Anyhow, no doubt these firms will learn the basics of advertising eventually. They certainly have the money. Four years ago, I was talking to Price Waterhouse in New York. One of their legion of VPs told me a million-dollar fee was small change even for one of their smaller divisions, so they can afford to plaster the globe with messages. But if you really want to know, the best business-to-business medium is direct mail – about four times as effective as trade advertising – though I believe in that too.

I hope they find agencies who know what they're doing, which you might imagine would mean direct marketing agencies – after all, they count their results and should know what works. I doubt it though, looking at most of the stuff they run for themselves. Brann, one of the largest firms, ran an ad the other week with the headline 'Ship Hot', a play on words as tasteless as it is irrelevant.

Why do agencies that make their living by getting responses for clients run ads that will do nothing of the sort for themselves? Perhaps, reverting to my topic of professional firms, the old legal maxim applies: the lawyer who acts for himself has a fool for a client. Some of their writers should spend time poring over John Watson's *Creativity in Direct Marketing*, probably the best recent English text on what works and what doesn't in ads. It will be much more help than weak puns.

□ □ □

DATE: OCTOBER 1998

BLOCKED TOILETS AND PRINTED GARBAGE

'Nothing kills a bad product faster than good advertising,' said Bill Bernbach. Actually, I think nothing kills a bad product faster than pissing money away, which brings me to the subject of my local railway station and the deplorable antics that have been taking place there.

If you have a long memory, and have bravely persisted with this column, you may recall a heart-rending tale I told four years ago. Whoever ran the station then had spent £500,000 tarting it up. As part of this grand piece of public work, they blocked up the splendid old lavatories, putting new ones inside the booking hall, which they locked thoughtfully every day after 1 o'clock, thus forcing me one night to take a furtive leak behind the local garage.

> The managements of these firms model their service not around us, but around their own rapacity, raising prices and cutting service whenever they can get away with it.

To keep costs down the station stayed largely unmanned, so vandals smashed most of the windows. They were then boarded up – not a cheap exercise. To this you can now add the extra it is costing to put in new glass. This will be smashed repeatedly, unless some great intellect realizes it would be cheaper to have someone there night and day than keep coughing up all this money.

But railway people are pretty adept at pissing away money, as I noticed when buying my ticket the other morning. Near the counter was a pile of glossy Great Western brochures that must have cost at least £1 each. The title was 'Our Disabled Persons Protection Policy'. 'Ah ha,' I said to myself. 'Interesting. They are selling insurance.'

But no: the brochures were about what the railway is doing for disabled people. The booking clerk, an amiable chap as bemused as me, said he'd received three boxes of them and in over two weeks just three copies had been taken. This wasteful exercise in fatuous self-congratulation is paid for out of the (fast-rising) fares. If they want to tell disabled people about these services, a simple poster, with a clear title like 'How we help disabled people', will do the trick.

I also picked up a leaflet headed 'We're modelling our service around you'. Inside is a lot of crap about their 'commitment to providing services which are fast, frequent and on time', 'service which is second to none' and 'fast and efficient access' (unless you want to take a leak). There is a handy English word for this stuff. It is 'lying'. Their services are getting slower, less frequent and more delayed. The one thing good about Great Western is the staff, who don't deserve to have their efforts, and their wages, belittled in this way.

The managements of these firms model their service not around us, but around their own rapacity, raising prices and cutting service whenever they can get away with it. We should string up the rascals who have just made fortunes behaving in such a foolish and grasping way, take their money and give it to those who have to live with the consequences every day – travellers and staff. And shoot the conniving politicians who made it possible, while we're about it.

NOTE: Since I wrote this, a report came out revealing that the railways in Britain, besides being dirty, unpunctual and badly run by shameless profiteers, are the most expensive in the world.

□ □ □

DATE: SEPTEMBER 1998

DOES THIS MAKE SENSE TO YOU?

The other morning I shaved with toothpaste, an aberration that will happily confirm many readers' views that I am going gaga. Marketing is a young person's game, so few of you will empathize with me. However the cause of my behaviour will not be entirely surprising to those of riper years.

If you have been blessed with good eyesight you may be somewhat alarmed to discover, usually in your 40s, that you start finding it hard to read fine print, particularly in soft lighting. That's why you sometimes see diners of a certain vintage holding restaurant menus not at the normal distance but about three feet away from their eyes.

> **F**irms take over others with much 'strategic' piffle about 'rationalization' and 'economies of scale'... firing some of the people who do the work and giving more to those who remain.

I don't know what the medical term is, but something nasty has happened to your retina and eventually you have to get either glasses or contact lenses or, if you are very bold, have laser surgery. So that is how I came to pick up a small tube of what I thought was shaving cream and smear it generously all over my face before noticing a pleasing peppermint aroma which persuaded me I had the wrong tube.

You may ask why I wasn't wearing my glasses. The answer is simple: I was lolling in the bath at the time, in which circumstance they steam up. Happily the toothpaste frothed up almost as well as shaving cream – and I carried on anyhow, doing a great job, whilst thinking how wonderful modern consumer products are.

Short-sightedness is not the sole province of decrepit writers, I reflected on reading an item in the 23 May issue about Rimmel, which nestled appropriately beside a piece by Mr and Mrs Snoddy's little lad about down-sizing, a subject we both agree about.

When I was young, Rimmel sold cheap cosmetics in Woolworths – and for all I know still do. They've just been taken over by Benckiser, the first casualties being marketing director Ann Hunter and managing director Jeff Peasland. It's always sad to see people lose their jobs, though one is hardly surprised to see it in this case. Invariably firms take over others with much 'strategic' piffle about 'rationalization' and 'economies of scale', or as I would put it, firing some of the people who do the work and giving more to those who remain.

Benckiser people are now going to do the two departees' jobs. Margaret Donnelly, marketing director of their fragrance company, Coty, will do Ms Hunter's, whilst Peasland's role has been added to the duties of Coty MD, Robin Linklater. Two possibilities emerge. Either the two people who have been handed these additional roles were previously loafing around all day with not enough to do or they are about to be seriously overworked.

Hard work is not a bad idea, but it is if people are too snowed under to do their jobs properly, and things go wrong. This is particularly true in direct marketing where detail is so critical. This macho mania for firing everyone in sight is crazy. What sense does it make to save maybe £80,000–£100,000 of pay plus the associated overheads yet jeopardize the effective expenditure of millions?

NOTE: Mr and Mrs Snoddy's offspring is the eminent media correspondent of *The Times*, whose talent and stamina are such that he has been writing for *Marketing* for even longer than I have.

□ □ □

DATE: JUNE 1996

FLOATING SUSPICIONS

In my extreme youth the Battle of Britain took place. The atmosphere was not unlike that during the recent football-fest, except the British behaved better, many in those far-off days having been taught good manners, and none having had their minds polluted by the propaganda the *Sun*, *Mirror* and so on now spew out.

To make steering difficult for the *Luftwaffe*, the skies were full of barrage balloons – called blimps nowadays – a sight I recalled three weekends ago when one was hovering over my London squat. On its side I could just read 'MasterCard'. You may judge this a fitting and ingenious wheeze, but I must be honest with you and reveal what flashed through my mind when I saw this ungainly vehicle: 'What silly bastard decided to do that?' Perhaps you consider this an overly harsh and peremptory response, so I will elaborate.

> Though some repetition is essential in advertising, any proposed message that tells people things they already know... should be viewed with deep suspicion.

Good marketing should, in so far as we frail humans can manage, match the resource to the need. Or to put it another way, you shouldn't waste money. Every penny squandered by lazy thinkers or vainglorious agencies on frivolous or irrelevant messages is a penny you could use to improve the product, cut the price or enhance the service: all much more important to the customer, who pays our wages. Therefore, though some repetition is essential in advertising, any proposed message that tells people things they already know in a boring way should be viewed with deep suspicion, and then cancelled without ceremony.

You may divide all markets into three stages. The first is when the kind of product is new and few customers know what it is, for example you offer the first ever credit card. The second is when the kind of product is no longer new, you have competitors, and customers are starting to understand what a credit card is. And the third is when everyone knows what a credit card is, and you have lots of competition.

In the first stage you must explain what a credit card is, how it is better than alternatives, and make people 'aware' of your brand. In the second you also have to show why yours is better than other brands. And in the third you need waste little effort explaining what a credit card does, but rather persuade customers to choose or keep choosing yours. That is where MasterCard is now.

This is, I'm sure, like mothers' milk to perceptive marketers like you, dear reader, but I seriously wonder how many people give it enough, or any, thought. A surprising number clearly think that no matter what stage the market is in, numbing repetition of the brand name – preferably in large letters – is all it takes to get results. I cannot believe the name 'MasterCard' is unknown to the wealthy Chelsea-ites whose houses face me across the river or even the poor folk on my side. And it is equally inconceivable that reminders – even on dirigibles – will make either group more likely to choose MasterCard, or indeed do anything save feel vaguely confused by this aerial tomfoolery.

A powerful, fairly complete competitive argument is a much better bet. Hot air is not enough.

NOTE: This effusion produced a furious counterblast from someone at MasterCard, which I then responded to – see page 169. As one journalist once remarked, if you are clever enough, your readers will write your columns for you.

□ □ □

DATE: JULY 1996

HOW FINANCIAL ADS OUGHT TO BE

The US talk-show demagogue Rush Limbaugh, whose politics are worryingly adjacent to those of the late Genghis Khan, has written two best-sellers whose titles are, I suspect, distinctly better than their content: *The Way Things Ought To Be* and *There, I Told You So*.

The latter sums up my reaction when *Campaign* magazine reported research a while ago showing customers see financial ads as 'condescending, patronizing and unrealistic'. I have been saying this for years. Banks especially have run some dire tripe. The exception, I suppose, is Lloyds, whose work has at least been consistent and well produced, but too many have followed the Goebbels

What they should work at is better products and service leading to better propositions, which should then be conveyed clearly.

paradigm: never mind the facts, just lie repeatedly – 'the bank that says "yes"', 'the action bank', 'the listening bank', when we know banks are too often negative, sluggish and deaf to all but profit.

Just about the only outstanding work I recall was over 20 years ago by John Webster and Brian Mindel for a bank that doesn't even exist any more, the National Provincial. It focused neatly on how direct debit made paying your bills less painful.

Other advertisers prance through never-never land, hoping to make themselves lovable, perhaps. Thirty-second epics dramatize the stunning revelation (no doubt derived from costly research) that their staff and customers are human; romantic ballads hymn early morning withdrawals from cash machines; buffoonish clerics dance with Dickensian quacks; ballet dancers cosy up improbably to heavy-metal musicians; neo-Busby Berkeley choreography is pressed into irrelevant service; they've even tried dull slogans printed back to front.

I was yakking about this last year at a direct marketing course attended by a young man from Nat West. One of his colleagues later rang me to ask why I thought their full page ads with drawings of people in deck chairs were about as much use as burning large piles of £5 notes. Alas, I had just lunched well and was less than entirely coherent.

What I should have said was that good advertising fits its subject. Money isn't warm, cuddly or funny. It's a serious matter, about numbers and practicalities, not images. What are your charges? How do your interest rates compare? How quickly can I get a loan? Do you offer a 100 per cent mortgage? Boring but necessary matters – hardly surprising, because banks are boring but necessary.

I don't want to love my bank, insurer or building society; I don't even want to like them. What I want is more cash and better service. I care about what they do, not what they claim. What they should work at is better products and service leading to better propositions, which should then be conveyed clearly. I suspect financial people, deep down, know this but have been led astray by the My Little Pony-tail brigade. They should trust their instincts.

A worthy example to emulate is M & G. No silly pictures, recycled pop tunes or misleading promises: just no-nonsense stuff, full of facts and numbers, in print not broadcast, so people can study the details. It must work: it's been running for ever.

NOTE: I'm afraid you won't remember many of the advertising examples I give in this piece – they were that bad. But you get the idea, I'm sure, because the same sort of rubbish still appears.

Interestingly enough, someone from M & G rang me up not long afterwards because they were thinking of changing their successful formula. This is almost always a mistake. Marketers get bored with their advertising long before customers do.

☐ ☐ ☐

DATE: FEBRUARY 1995

IS FINANCE THAT SIMPLE? I WONDER

Have you ever felt ashamed at being attracted to some gruesome sight despite yourself? Road accidents, for example, always draw horrified yet fascinated onlookers. I know this from personal experience: at 18 I was run over and nearly died. Indeed, I was an object of medical curiosity as the first person in the north of England known to survive a ruptured liver. I recall vividly feeling oppressed by the circle of gawpers pressing in.

I am often drawn in an analogous way to the antics of meretricious entertainers with an engaging way of saying nothing in particular. Jimmy Saville was one. Chris Evans is another. Not long ago he mentioned a glorious invention

> There is a world of difference between fooling around with money and fooling around with groceries.

that can only hearten those of us who believe progress is still possible in this wicked world. The breakthrough in question is the polypropylene artificial testicle for dogs or rather, since these things tend to come in pairs, polypropylene artificial testicles. These have been introduced in the United States, of course – where life at its best and worst is to be seen – to assuage the post-operative trauma of male dogs who have had their own removed. It all reminds me of the touching riddle: how many country and western singers does it take to change a light bulb? Five – one to change the old one, the other four to sing about the one they lost.

In an age when such marvels are possible, what can we say about our petty struggles in marketing? Take the great supermarket war, in which the antagonists, exhausted from struggling over their traditional turf, have sought to change the battleground, first launching competing schemes of bribery and now moving into things like banking. In my view, the bankers couldn't possibly be as bad as people paint them, but if I ran supermarkets I would think hard before allying myself with people who find their own business so tough – either because they might screw things up in mine, or because anything as difficult to do well as banking may not be a good business to enter. It's not as simple as pumping petrol, for example.

There is a world of difference between fooling around with money and fooling around with groceries. What is more there are sometimes signs that these new ventures are undertaken as a way of escaping unpleasant reality, rather as prime ministers become engrossed by foreign policy when everything at home goes pear-shaped.

For instance, a ton of money and thought has been invested in enlarging and improving my local Sainsbury's. When the grand opening occurred, magnificently choreographed in stages, maps were given out to show you where everything was, and a small army of people appeared to direct you. Despite all this planning in a business Sainsbury's know very well, it was impossible for some weeks to find something in their kitchen section you would think any fool would know is essential to anybody fitting out a kitchen: a small knife for cutting things.

If something that simple is hard to do, I wonder how good they'll be at banking. We shall see.

NOTE: On reflection, I may have been wrong here. Since many of the banks are so bad at what they do, perhaps the supermarkets can do better. Then again, as I write Sainsbury's are having a very hard time – as are Marks & Spencer.

□ □ □

DATE: DECEMBER 1996

PULL THE OTHER ONE, GUV

Nobody, not even your thick-skinned columnist, likes being told he is an idiot, so you can imagine how carefully I read the letter from Richard Busby on 2 July, castigating my folly in taking on the $16.5 billion global sponsorship industry, of which he is clearly a proud member, by criticizing World Cup sponsorship.

His arguments – tinged, I fear, by self-interest – were neither novel nor susceptible to examination. First, he said that such a lot of money is spent on such promotions that they must be a good idea, a line of thinking which can be applied with equal force to land-mines, or for that matter crack cocaine. Second (many people have been at pains to point this out to me before), he thinks I am too stupid to understand these elevated matters. What sponsorship buys, he explained with infinite patience as to a small child, is the 'acquisition of the rights of association'. And third, the return on investment derives from the way this sort of thing is exploited in the 'marketing mix'.

> **M**ost of the £600 million invested in World Cup links was probably wasted... I am not saying sponsorship is bad; I am just saying it should be relevant and carefully thought out.

But the eager scrutiny I gave to his comments was nothing to that I applied to reports showing that most of the £600 million invested in World Cup links was probably wasted. It seems the 12 official sponsors of France 98 put up £250 million in order to render two-thirds of viewers unable to remember their names and 55 per cent to get them wrong. So this, I said to myself, is what Mr Busby was trying to explain to silly old me: you spend £50 million and nobody associates you with anything. Actually that's unfair: there were more complaints about Vauxhall's nasty little sponsorship spots than anything else. As for the 'marketing mix', how do you exploit something most of your customers are blissfully unaware of? Beats me.

Over a century ago, a man deeply in debt asked one of the Rothschilds to lend him some money. The response was 'No, but I will walk across the floor of the London stock exchange arm in arm with you.' Now **that** was the intelligent use of a natural association, but the things I was discussing – Citibank and Elton John, for instance – do not seem natural partners. Mr Busby did mention the Co-op bank, which I admire greatly, but I cannot see why, as they were not World Cup sponsors to my knowledge.

His point that promotions make people change their buying habits is quite true. Unfortunately, though, what bribes give, bribes take away. When your promotion ends, someone else's begins. Many did indeed go to Sainsbury's to collect their David Beckham medals, but most are now drifting back to the supermarket they started with.

You could say I was underwhelmed by Mr Busby's arguments, but they did give me a few good laughs, which is more than those who blew £600 million have enjoyed. I am not saying sponsorship is bad; I am just saying it should be relevant and carefully thought out – and if this is the level of thinking Mr Busby employs in his pitches to likely punters I would be very careful before succumbing to his blandishments.

□ □ □

DATE: JULY 1998

THE BALANCE OF TERROR

My financial dealings over the years have been eclectic, eccentric and, let's not mince words, stunningly incompetent. I have made a living in the most bizarre ways, some of which you might find hard to believe – like selling malt whisky for investment on the phone, pop records through Swedish newsagents and swimming pool franchises in France. The tangles I have got into from time to time with Her Majesty's Commissioners of Inland Revenue are too depressing to recount here but would certainly elevate a few eyebrows amongst those of you who know how to manage your affairs.

Despite this, finance fascinates me, which is why I was recently chuckling over an article in *The Economist* about auditors. Some, it seems, are being sued for spectacular sums by clients who feel they have received bad advice. One is facing a demand for £105 million dam-

> You have probably noticed how many reasons other than advertising an agency can blame for fiscal disasters in a client's business.

ages. Not surprisingly the partners in these firms, who are of course accountants and not noted for their sense of adventure save with other people's money, have been seeking ways to evade their individual responsibilities. They want to change the law. *The Economist* pooh-poohed this. They felt that as long as auditors are keenly aware of the consequences of their actions they will approach their task with 'a healthy sense of terror'.

This splendid phrase made me think. Why cannot the same principle be applied to our business, where all agencies pose as 'professional'? Many clients I speak to complain that their agencies are dictatorial and full of amazing certainty when telling them what to do, but pay no penalty and indeed are rarely even upbraided when their certainties produce slumping sales.

We all know it is often impossible to isolate what part the advertising plays in your marketing, though I've noticed that whenever a firm does enjoy success the agency is very quick to claim the credit. Conversely, you have probably noticed how many reasons other than advertising an agency can blame for fiscal disasters in a client's business. Despite this the only sanction you can generally apply is that of changing agencies. Particularly amusing in this context is the way many financial institutions have changed their agencies without to my mind noticeably improving their advertising.

And what about direct marketing, where results are measurable? I was addressing an audience at one firm a while ago. When to their relief I ended after trotting out my usual selection of droll examples, pithy exhortations and off-colour jokes, one executive came up and said, 'Maybe we should talk about doing business,' to which I responded amiably, 'What a good idea. I suppose you'd like to get higher responses to your mailings,' to which came the lugubrious response, 'We'd be happy to get any response at all.'

I don't know if a healthy sense of terror is the answer, but a little more humility might help. A while ago I asked someone whose talents I admire what motivated him. 'Fear of failure,' he replied. I do so agree. That, and reflecting before we boldly go for another so-called creative breakthrough that someone else's money, someone else's business and someone else's career are on the line.

□ □ □

DATE: MARCH 1996

YOU CAN BANK ON IT

Christopher Fildes, that very funny financial journalist, has a joke he likes so much he trots it out regularly. 'Giving money to a bank is like giving a gallon of beer to a drunk. You know what he's going to do with it. You're just not sure which wall it'll end up against.'

I thought of this recently when thinking about whoever dispenses HSBC Midland Bank's advertising money so generously. I was analysing one of their ads to work out how it manages to be so ill-conceived in almost every respect.

It features a stylish shot of a lady with her infant daughter, romping in carefree mode on the beach. I imagine this is meant to convey the insouciant joy of one with no money worries, though research shows if you show people on beaches readers naturally think about holiday resorts.

> **A**lmost everybody selling financial services promises us to arrange things so we never have to worry again. This is about as credible as a politician's promises.

Three headlines fight for your attention. The first cannot possibly gain it, as it is carefully placed over the sand of the beach so you can't read it. Just as well, really, as it is incomprehensibly twee. It reads: 'Money says, "But you still haven't opened those bank statements, have you?"' Just the sort of thing little girls say to mum on holiday. Or is it mum saying it to the little girl? Or is it God? Who cares?

Sadly the next headline, which you can read, is staggeringly unoriginal in both concept and language. It says, 'Let's sort money out.' Almost everybody selling financial services promises us to arrange things so we never have to worry again. This is about as credible as a politician's promises, since they never explain precisely how this miracle will be wrought.

The copy begins, 'At times like this, bank statements should be the last thing on your mind.' Not bad: two clichés in one sentence. This is followed by an infallible sign of bad writing – a change of person – because that sentence talks about 'your money' whereas the next runs, 'That's why we need to keep money under control.' (I like the idea of keeping money 'under control'. One pictures it as a kind of ravening beast, likely to savage people at dead of night if not kept in.) The third sentence reverts to the second person, 'Checking your account balance regularly is one way...'.

In the third headline a good idea creeps in: 'a free book to help you take control of money'. This 'practical and impartial guide will help you put money in its place and help you enjoy real peace of mind'. How nice: another cliché.

Apart from knowing zip about how pictures communicate and managing headlines, the art director doesn't know what gets response. The coupon is carefully placed so as to be ignored – in a thin anaemic strip at the bottom. I know – to ensure 'the integrity of the design' was not 'compromised'.

Lord knows how much they're squandering on this stuff. If they looked at return on investment, someone would have an immediate heart arrest.

And, I might add, this applies with even greater force to the current wave of expenditure on changing the name of the Midland Bank, which at least has some meaning, to the initials HSBC, which have none.

NOTE: Shortly after this appeared, Lloyds Bank spent a fortune changing the look of all their branches, stationery and so on. Imagine what would happen if they applied the same money and enthusiasm to improving their service. Unlikely, though.

□ □ □

DATE: MARCH 1999

WHAT'S WRONG WITH ADVERTISING?

Introduction

When I started in advertising, people were just starting to talk about marketing and something else called 'merchandising', almost interchangeably.

Nobody quite knew what they were, but merchandising was something to do with getting your products displayed and promoted better, I seem to recall. It's barely mentioned nowadays. This seems a shame, since – as you will gather from a few of these pieces – ignorance is no barrier to success in our little world.

But the keenest protagonists of marketing were the advertising agencies; and the most visible even glamorous part of marketing is unquestionably advertising. It is the thing people get most excited about; it attracts more rewards, more money and perhaps more talent than any other aspect of marketing.

Marketing has only been talked about for 40 or 50 years. But advertising is certainly very old. I saw one of the earliest advertisements when I went to the Greek city of Ephesus. It is a sign leading to the local brothel, which seems fitting somehow, and must be about 2,000 years old.

So you would think that by now people would pretty well understand how to go about advertising. Indeed, there is no reason why they shouldn't, for a great many clever people have devoted a ton of time and energy into understanding what makes it work.

They do not entirely agree among themselves, but certain principles are quite clear, almost as clear as the fact that hardly anybody who creates or pays for it feels the need to discover what they are. And that is why you see so much appalling advertising.

HOW TO ADVERTISE

Do you know how to advertise? What a silly question. Of course you do.

First, you extract as much money as you can from the people in charge, based on any of a number of vague criteria. These almost certainly don't include the only sensible one – the long-term value of a customer – because you don't know it.

Then you spend weeks, even months talking to good-looking, persuasive people from ad agencies about your plans. Finally you choose the one that seems best, usually on the evidence of elaborate and detailed proposals from people who cannot possibly understand your business. If you have a big budget you will garner from this tiresome and confusing process a photo in this or another magazine accompanied by wildly misleading information about how you arrived at your decision and a few words of vile sycophancy from your new agency's boss.

> Then, 9 times out of 10, the speculative campaign that so enchanted you will be discarded as impractical, and you will never see the people who did it.

Then, 9 times out of 10, the speculative campaign that so enchanted you will be discarded as impractical, and you will never see the people who did it. They will be working on another new business pitch, as will the charmers you met, and you'll be handed over to the oily rags who will do the real work.

You may wonder if they know what they're doing, because a few months later you'll either be collecting awards and a bonus, or the addresses of good executive search agencies. In fact, do you ever wonder if **you** know what you're doing? I don't ask that maliciously, because most people have very little idea. A few years ago, when David Ogilvy was asked for his advice by James D Robinson III, the (about to be fired) head of American Express, he said, 'Why don't you hire someone who understands advertising?'

These thoughts are provoked by re-reading an excellent book called *How to Advertise*, given to me years ago by one of the authors, Ken Roman, former head of the Ogilvy Group. It will save you a vast amount of indecision, heartache and financial disaster, because it covers a huge range of topics clearly and with admirable brevity. They include weighty matters like why, when and how often you should change a campaign, which media suit which products and false assumptions about integration. But they also include wise words on lesser, but still perplexing subjects like what research reveals about jingles, the right way to read a radio script, what to bear in mind when using a celebrity and how big the letters should be on your posters.

The book has been revised and reissued as *The New How to Advertise*. You'll be impressed by how well it is written, which is why you should do yourself a huge favour and buy *Writing that Works*, also by Ken, but with a different collaborator, Joel Raphaelson. It is the best and shortest book on how to write good business English. Give it to your staff: it could save you countless tedious hours trying to wrench sense from their sloppy prose.

☐ ☐ ☐

DATE: OCTOBER 1998

I DON'T THINK THAT'S FUNNY, DO YOU?

One of my creative partners, Phil Brisk, who lives in quaint but gritty Saddleworth – *Last of the Summer Wine* country – showed me a piece in the *Guardian* recently. 'No jokes, please, we're German, advertising students told', said the headline.

It seems an expert was advising would-be advertising people to avoid merry quips if they want to sell to their countrymen, who, he revealed, aren't motivated by that sort of thing. In Britain, on the other hand, the article pointed out, funny ads work very well. Since most of the world has long believed the Germans have no sense of humour, whereas the British almost own the copyright, this came as no surprise.

> The problem with humour comes when it is irrelevant... or where the jokes are so good you can't remember what was advertised.

But humour is a funny old thing. Twenty-eight years ago my partner and I had a spectacularly unsuccessful business in Sweden, another place where humour is allegedly in scant supply. Some Swedes seemed almost ashamed about this. A surprising number were at pains to tell me that whereas all their countrymen were stone-faced oafs, they themselves were always game for a laugh. All I can say is that when our business went broke, none of the creditors found it at all hilarious. I wasn't exactly chortling with glee myself, for that matter.

It is over 70 years since Claude Hopkins, perhaps the most able advertising man ever, ruled that 'no man buys from a clown' in his *Scientific Advertising*, which is perhaps the best advertising book ever. Yet humour often sells – even in Germany. I have in my files some funny ads for a German mail-order catalogue firm, believe it or not, which did very well. One offered a free washing machine to all families with more than 13 children, saying everyone else would have to buy one, and ending with the price plus instructions on how to order.

It sold loads of washing machines and made audiences in many countries laugh – especially in places like India, where they have large families. The campaign featured a number of similar offers, such as free baby clothes for all families who had had twins that week and a free tracksuit for all readers over 7 feet tall. Its aim was to make the firm, which was seen as just another impersonal monolith, seem more human, and to sell goods at the same time. It achieved both objectives.

The problem with humour comes when it is irrelevant, or where what the creators think is funny is either not funny or even plain stupid to most of the audience, or where the jokes are so good you can't remember what was advertised. One good example is the appallingly unfunny press advertising used to launch First Direct. Another is that hilarious old campaign featuring Leonard Rossiter and Joan Collins, which I think was for Cinzano, but I'm not sure – and nor were many of the people who saw it.

This sort of thing usually happens because creative people are showing off. As Claude Hopkins also said, 'Instead of sales, they seek applause.' Nowadays this means awards, of course.

NOTE: One problem with humour is not only that what you find funny I don't, it is also that it doesn't travel very well. As marketers try to transfer successful campaigns from one market to another, this makes it very hard to use. I have been telling jokes for 20 years all over the world, just to make my speeches a little less boring. For what it is worth, I find that ones about marriage, money and bad driving tend to be well received almost everywhere.

□ □ □

DATE: AUGUST 1998

OF TORTOISES AND OTHER MATTERS

I suppose many of you are, like me, entertained by Auberon Waugh's writing. But funny as he is, I don't think he is a match for his father Evelyn who, before writing novels, wrote on travel, art and architecture. Here is a thoughtful observation he made about an unusual, but rather unsatisfying shipboard race in 1929: 'The chief disability suffered by tortoises as racing animals is not slowness, so much as a poor sense of direction.'

It seems to me the chief disability suffered by many if not most marketers is not sloth, so much as poor grasp of priorities. Too often they feel fiddling with trivia will solve basic problems; in particular they seem to imagine bullshit is a

> **I**f the generic product... is popular, you can often do very well without advertising at all, as long as you have good packaging, distribution and display.

substitute for action. A good example is the current Barclays Bank campaign. Besides being needlessly obscure it offers little or no competitive benefit to the prospect – and the same can be said of many other advertisers.

I have quoted in these columns before my favourite definition of marketing, from a long-dead American millionaire: 'Find out what people want and need, and give it to them – and you'll get rich', a much snappier description than the CIM's multisyllabic one. It is instructive, then, to examine the activities of the Cott Corporation. They are the Canadian chaps, you recall, who came over here not long ago and wrought havoc in the cola market.

Amazingly enough their secret is rather old-fashioned. A good example is a beer they formulated in Canada called 'President's Reserve'. They started by analysing how the best beers in the world – which of course come from Pilsen – are brewed, and comparing them with what was available in

Canada. They then set about brewing a better beer using superior ingredients and methods. They imported hops twice as expensive as the ones used by other Canadian brewers; they matured the beer for 50 per cent longer; they conducted taste tests; and, lo and behold, people liked it. Because it wasn't advertised, they could sell it for less. Within a few months they had 2 per cent of the Canadian beer market.

There is a moral in this. If the generic product – in this case beer – is popular, you can often do very well without advertising at all, as long as you have good packaging, distribution and display. If the reality is good enough, you'll succeed. Marks & Spencer are a good example. I'm not saying advertising is not a good idea – on average those firms that advertise most are most profitable – but it is sometimes possible to thrive without it.

Conversely, advertising cannot change reality. This should be pointed out to the people who, I read a while ago, have decided to run advertising to persuade people to use those maddening cardboard cartons, now outdated by new ones with easy pouring mechanisms.

I learnt this lesson as a callow – well, all right, thoroughly obnoxious – youth, when the practice by men of wearing hats was going out of fashion. For years and years enormous sums were poured into an advertising campaign with the beguiling line, 'If you want to get ahead, get a hat.' It didn't help the hat industry, or indeed the head industry for that matter. The agency did quite well, though, as usual.

NOTE: I apologize, but the Barclays Bank campaign I refer to was actually so obscure that I can't remember a thing about it, which itself makes a point, I suppose.

The CIM – the Chartered Institute of Marketing – defines marketing as a discipline that 'identifies, anticipates and satisfies customer needs at a profit'.

The Cott Corporation helped one or two supermarket chains improve their cola offerings, and the sales results gave the big brands a big fright.

□ □ □

DATE: SEPTEMBER 1995

ON DIFFICULT CLIENTS

The careful management of clients is a rare skill, with which I was, alas, not blessed at birth. J Walter Thompson, however, clearly was. Once he was looking at a picture of a kitten prepared for a client. 'That is the best picture of a kitten I have ever seen,' he said to the artist. 'Just paint a large red bow on it round the kitten's neck – like this.' The man protested: it would practically hide the creature's face. Thompson said, 'That's the idea. The client will notice that and suggest it be removed, thinking it was all his own idea.'

Not long ago Winston Fletcher suggested agencies are nothing but a bunch of whingers complaining about clients' unreasonable ways. A week later, Raoul Pinnell was saying how badly agencies managed their businesses. Having run a couple of agencies, starting with my own money – or to be honest no money at all in one case, just ample desperation – I yield to none in my incompetence. On the other hand clients are exceedingly difficult to manage, often because they mess you around so much.

> **D**avid Ogilvy used to have a sign in his office reading 'Please, God: send us smart clients.'

Years ago, IBM screwed us around so remorselessly, if unintentionally, that I asked for a meeting and said to the client as politely as I could, 'Either you pay us a whole lot more money or I'm afraid we can't do business any more.' IBM was then (about 16 years ago) perhaps the most highly regarded firm in the world, and he said something like, 'You can't say that to IBM,' to which I replied, 'I just did' – not having heard that wonderful phrase, 'Read my lips.'

I tried to explain. 'It has taken us a deal of time, trouble and effort to put together our staff. Talent is hard to come by, but in our industry, which is a new one, it is even harder. The other day an art director came in to me in tears because she had found seven different sets of amendments on one piece of your finished artwork. If I can get enough good people like her, I can always get more of you; the reverse does not apply.'

If you enjoy cultural footnotes, here is how a client treated someone with infinitely more talent than anyone in advertising today – Botticelli's rival, Domenico Ghirlandaio. His amazingly demanding contract in 1485 with Fra Bernardo of the Spedale Monastery for an altarpiece covered expenses and even told him which paint to use. It said, 'He must colour the panel at his own expense with good colours and with powdered gold on such orna-ments as demand it… the blue must be ultramarine of the value about four florins the ounce.' He would be paid '115 large florins if it seems to me, the said Fra Bernardo, that it is worth it'.

I'm told David Ogilvy used to have a sign in his office reading 'Please, God: send us smart clients.' The client is the boss – rightly. But you can't beat having one that's educated. Fra Bernardo clearly knew a bit about painting.

☐ ☐ ☐

DATE: FEBRUARY 1998

POSTERMANIA

Your columnist is a jovial soul cursed with an embarrassingly loud laugh that is often criticized cruelly by his spouse and usually engendered by manifestations of the absurd. And where better to find them than in the world of the poster? Nowadays what was once high art sanctified by Mucha and Toulouse-Lautrec often seems the responsibility of people who are either not too clever, or lazy, or both.

How often do they give thought to the circumstances under which their concoctions will be seen? Take some Safeway posters a client helpfully told me about which said, 'You know where to go.' They were in Weybridge, Surrey; the stores were in Chalk Farm, Queensbury and Brent Cross. I may know where to go, but why on earth should I drive clear across Greater London to get there?

> **T**his should lead the intelligent person to assume that good posters must be simple, striking and understandable in a split second.

Folly often rules amongst the displays near my London hovel. Some confuse good advertising with bad puns, like the one for Nokia featuring a moony-faced nun and priest: 'A superior way to talk to mother' is the pathetic quip employed. Others have clearly been dreamt up with no reference to the fact that almost all those exposed to them are whizzing past in their shiny little motor cars, far more intent on not hitting other shiny little motor cars than looking at posters. This should lead the intelligent person to assume that good posters must be simple, striking and understandable in a split second.

How, then, is one to fathom the thinking behind a current poster for Rutland? Looking remarkably similar to the campaign for the London Zoo, this deploys a droll picture of a chicken called Simone to illustrate the old rustic joke, 'We had to close the zoo when the chicken died', selected no doubt because Rutland used to be the smallest county in England. Quite funny. Unfortunately chickens, zoos, jokes and Rutland are not being sold, but that excellent ale, Ruddles. However, since neither the brand name nor the beer is all that prominent, you would never know it as you race to the office.

And what about the production I saw last week, which features a muscular, oiled male torso in the manner now *de rigueur* in jeans commercials? He is doing something obscure with a huge spanner to the insides of what looks like a giant wristwatch, though a friend says it's a turbine. The line says, 'Labour would really benefit from a better health policy.' I immediately assumed the lads at Conservative Central Office had gone doolally until I saw in small thin lettering on the top right hand of the poster the words 'Foundation Health'. Nothing to do with jeans, Labour, watches or turbines. In fact nothing to do with anything.

But I could not fault the bold placement of this poster – diagonally opposite one of London's leading gay nighteries. Even though it cannot conceivably do anything for the client, perhaps it will raise a few smiles amongst tired revellers as they totter off home at three in the morning.

□ □ □

DATE: JUNE 1995

SHOULD THEY GET AWAY WITH IT?

'Madam, you have between your legs an instrument capable of giving immense pleasure, but you sit there scratching at it,' said Sir Thomas Beecham to the cellist. Besides being a notable wag Beecham had a dictatorial way with orchestras. When I saw him conducting in my teens the best thing about the whole performance was him shouting at his players when they irked him.

His greatest memorial is the way he single-handedly promoted the music of Frederick Delius, who otherwise would probably have remained in obscurity. He was able to become a conductor because of wealth derived from Beecham's Pills, a remedy largely composed, I believe, of bicarbonate of soda and sold, in the carefree fashion then pursued by medical advertisers, as a remedy for just about everything from indigestion to cancer.

> Bill Bernbach once said, 'Nothing kills a bad product faster than good advertising.' Far worse in my view is advertising which makes claims that cannot be delivered.

They may not have done people much good but they did have the saving grace that compared to some competitors they didn't do much harm. A number of the competitors were largely composed of alcohol, and sometimes opium, thus guaranteeing that if you didn't become a drunk you probably became a drug addict. Terrifying when you think quite a few were actually recommended for babies.

Since then advertising has been regulated to make such claims and products impossible. Nobody today could promise 'Bio-Bilge will make you slim' or 'Juvasex will make you young again' without having to prove it. The one area where such sharp practice still flourishes unchecked is political advertising. I would love to think school classes will get smaller, hospital waiting lists shorter, as Labour posters promised – but how? Many of these things are controlled by forces no government commands. By what miracle could they summon out of thin air in any reasonable period the school teachers (let alone literate ones) needed to make classes smaller, or the doctors to make waiting lists shorter, even if the money existed, which it does not? Nor will more taxes produce that money as swiftly or copiously as politicians would like. The British public like every other will always find its way round tax demands when they exceed the reasonable.

I cannot believe anyone advertising a car, a washing machine, a credit card – or for that matter Beecham's Powders – would be allowed to get away with such unjustifiable claims. It is scandalous that politicians are permitted to make promises about our lives and our children's that, should they prove false, will affect us far more than any claims ordinary advertising might make. And what is going to happen when two years from now voters notice that these promises – on issues about which we have such strong feelings – have not been honoured?

Bill Bernbach once said, 'Nothing kills a bad product faster than good advertising.' Far worse in my view is advertising which makes claims that cannot be delivered. Politicians are expected to tell any lies they like to get elected. But do they have to bring their nasty practices into our relatively respectable field? The Government should do something about it. (Just kidding, really.)

NOTE: For once I was right. Almost exactly two years after this appeared, people began to become rather agitated about the promises made by the Labour Party.

These certainly helped to win the election. However, school class sizes went up, not down; hospital queues got longer, not shorter; and the promised 'ethical foreign policy' looked a little suspect when it was learnt we were selling arms to the corrupt and repressive Indonesian Government.

□ □ □

DATE: MAY 1997

SOME WEIRD STUFF GOING ON

I just got an envelope from Scottish Provident marked 'private and confidential'. For once the phrase was true, not just a sly trick to get me to open it, since it contained news about my pension fund, news **so** private and confidential that the letter inside was completely blank. Something wrong with the computer, I suppose; but I am often mystified by what people in this business do, and why.

An agency called tsm has been spending a lot of money on an ad headed 'The power of advertising with the **precision** of direct marketing'. They have a quixotic approach to getting a response: no name to reply to, nor any kind of request, urge, incentive or

> **A**s David Ogilvy pointed out many years ago, our job is not to make people say 'Wow'. It is to make them say, 'I'll buy that product.'

encouragement to do so. Rather sad, really: it's an admirably designed ad with an interesting proposition.

Mind you, Ken Humphrey, Bosch marketing communications manager, would make an ideal client for them. He's running ads with phone numbers, but with 'no immediate plans to use any data that is captured'. He's not even sure direct marketing would work in his sector – a 'pushy approach' on which 'the jury is still out'. Has he been cloistered in the depths of the Black Forest for the last decade? Doesn't he know every intelligent marketer in the world and even some not too bright are obsessed with data and what can be done with it?

Jon Ingall, about to be promoted to some grand, unspecified function in the HAVAS group would never make that mistake. But he did say in one of those adulatory interviews the trade press uses to fill blank pages, 'When was the last time you got something through the letterbox and said "Wow"?' As David Ogilvy pointed out many years ago, our job is not to make people say 'Wow'. It is to make them say, 'I'll buy that product.' What's more, since the latest DMIS research shows direct mail volumes have doubled in the last four years but readership has only dropped from 59 per cent to 58 per cent, somebody must be getting it right.

And who told the police to stick up posters with an arrow pointing down to the word 'burglary', boasting that rates are down? Having been burgled myself lately, I can tell you that news is a bad joke when you wait several hours for the police to come from a station only three or four miles away in a quiet country area. (We waited a whole day for the fingerprint man to come and over 24 hours for anyone to come and start detecting.) The news is not that special anyhow. A principal reason for lower crime rates lies in demographics. There aren't so many young thugs as there used to be. Bored police are reduced to spraying CS gas in the faces of badly parked old age pensioners.

Finally, what on God's green earth possesses easyJet to put the Go logo on their posters? Do they think that discourages people from travelling with Go? It builds awareness for them. An own goal of World Cup class.

NOTE: In another piece I tell the Go side of the easyJet story. It seems I was right.

□ □ □

DATE: JULY 1998

210

THE SAME OLD STORY

A woman with a rash on her hand goes to the doctor. The doctor looks at it closely but has no idea what it is. He looks out of the window thoughtfully, and then asks, 'Have you had this before?' The patient says, 'Yes.' 'I see,' says the doctor. Then, after another thoughtful pause, 'Well, you've got it again.'

That comes from Mark Twain, who was a damn sight funnier over a century ago than most comedians are today. And talking about comedians, we're in a recession again – quite inevitable, since all Labour governments confuse spending money with getting things done.

What can you, the intelligent marketer, do? The usual arguments are being aired. Firms must save money by cutting down on everything not essential, and that includes marketing if they see it as an expense, not an investment. A friend who runs a publisher's calls it 'saving your way to glory'.

> Today about 90 per cent of marketers have taken the first step towards effective advertising: they have put response devices in their advertisements.

Many advocate the opposite – increase or at least maintain spending – since in past recessions firms which did so emerged stronger than before. This appeals to marketers, of course, for eminently practical reasons like a keen desire to stay employed. But it also makes sense. If everyone else cuts down but you increase, you gain a disproportionate benefit. Even if you simply maintain spending at the same level whilst others reduce, you're going to come out better.

This sounds all very well, but it does not deal with ugly reality. You're short of cash, because your profits, from which you must first mollify your shareholders, and then fund everything else, are down. Who can conjure money out of thin air? The answer is: anyone who starts to spend his or her money wisely. This means behaving like a thrifty housewife: record the results of everything you do to the last penny, so as to find out what works and what doesn't, and then invest in the former rather than the latter.

Since the last recession something has happened which makes this much easier. Today about 90 per cent of marketers have taken the first step towards effective advertising: they have put response devices in their advertisements. They can see which ones work best, and which of the media in which they appear work best. But will they bother to do so?

Measurement is pointless if its lessons are ignored – and they probably will be if your agency has anything to do with it. Most have fought tooth and nail against including response devices; now they wriggle out of drawing any conclusions from the results. Many will discourage recording them at all. Here's the line – and I bet it's familiar to many of you – 'The ad isn't designed to get a response, but to build your image. The responses are just a bonus.'

Sheer poppycock. If people reply, they read or watched your ad with interest; and unless you think advertising works by osmosis, that must be your aim. 'When someone has read your ad, they want to know what to do,' said John Caples all those years ago. 'Tell them.'

□   □   □

DATE: NOVEMBER 1998

WHY IS SO MUCH ADVERTISING BAD?

'Tell young Drayton what happened when tha wife left thee, Alec' was a popular request in the vaults at my parents' pub, The Sycamore Inn, Ashton-under-Lyne. Alec's lugubrious response – 'She said she were going out just to get a loaf of bread, and I've never seen her since' – was always greeted with satisfied roars of laughter.

The assembled veterans never seemed to tire of it, though I believe the exchange took place in exactly the same words every time I served, quite illegally, behind the bar. The job was poorly paid, even though it was not always easy. Those old chaps were pernickety about their pint. On the one hand, it had to have a good head on it; on the other, if the top of the liquid were more than one-eighth of an inch below the top of the glass, pressing questions would be asked about why it was only half-full.

> Extensive research by Gallup some years ago showed that advertising that persistently focuses upon a competitive advantage does best.

Guinness for many years – and even to some extent now – made a great thing of the creamy head on their stout. One of the most famous advertising images ever is the smiling moon-face drawn on it in a poster that ran before the Second World War. And of course more recently Boddingtons has enjoyed astonishing success by focusing on what's on top of the beer rather than what's in it. Moreover just as the Guinness posters used both to sell and entertain, so does it work with Boddingtons today. It's a good example of the fact that the principles of advertising do not change.

These principles have been known since the early years of the century when US university professors like Hotchkiss, and brilliant practitioners like

Claude Hopkins explained them. But the evidence suggests most agency people and their clients are tragically unaware of them. How can this be? Are people too damned lazy to study? Or is nobody teaching them anyhow? It's all quite a puzzle.

If your advertising is to succeed, it is as well to pay attention to three questions. The first goes through every customer's mind when considering whether to buy something: 'Compared to what?' Springing from this are two subsidiaries: 'What can you do for me that nobody else can?' and 'Can you do something better for me than anyone else can?' Unless your ads address these points fully, they will probably fail. This is not just my opinion. Extensive research by Gallup some years ago showed that advertising that persistently focuses upon a competitive advantage does best.

But how much does? For instance, a recent (badly laid-out) P & O ad waffles on about paradise, which any holiday destination or cruise line could. Why did nobody pause to ask why anyone should take a cruise, and why with P & O in particular?

David Ogilvy used to say that unless your advertising contains a big idea, it will pass like a ship in the night. To this I would add that unless it shows why you are better, it will sink without trace.

□ □ □

DATE: MARCH 1998

WHY MERGERS ARE HELL

'We love him and want him to stay,' said 'Jo' Hoare plaintively next to a photo of Trevor Beattie, looking like a particularly dissolute Gypsy King. Beattie, you may recollect, resigned from his agency after its merger with TBWA. You wouldn't catch bankers talking about love like that – it might give rise to dark rumours. But such effusive affection is one thing that makes advertising such fun. Another is the crazy things people do, high on the list of which is merging agencies in the fond belief that the whole will be greater than the sum of the parts, when more often than not the reverse happens.

> **A** 10-year US study of mergers and acquisitions found that in 57 per cent of cases the firms ended up worth less together than separately.

BBD&O came over to Britain in the 50s and bought Dolan, Ducker, Whitcomb and Stewart. The owner, Pat Dolan, did pretty well, but BBD&O did not; they were an unhappy agency for years. They tried to spend themselves out of trouble again, buying Papert, Koenig & Lois, where oddly enough I once worked. No thanks to me, it was known as London's most creative agency, having amongst its alumni Alan Parker who now does quite well in films, and Peter Mayle who has also prospered, first from rude books about willies with Gray Jolliffe and then from respectable but funnier ones about France. Anyhow, that didn't work out, so BBD&O bought Samuels, Jones, Isaacson and Page. This also proved a failure; in fact they didn't get it right till they went in with AMV, wisely leaving them in control.

In the 60s O & M swallowed S H Benson, one of Britain's oldest, best-loved agencies. Horrifying tales came out; the Benson folk felt it was like being on the wrong side in the St Valentine's Day massacre. No surprise there: one of O & M's bosses then was a legendarily unpleasant creative director called Ellerington, who was, despite the name, actually a Rumanian.

A 10-year US study of mergers and acquisitions found that in 57 per cent of cases the firms ended up worth less together than separately. Many are driven not by good business thinking but by ego. The Saatchi & Saatchi debacle was a good example. And not a few are a substitute for sorting out either one or both of the businesses, rather like two drunks holding each other up on Saturday night. Financial people organize these deals. They just look at the figures. Little attention is paid to the culture of the firms involved, which often differs greatly – like two blood groups.

Advertising is still the main product agencies sell. Since Trevor Beattie was apparently responsible for the sprightly fusion of right execution with right message for the Nissan Micra, and for the outstanding Wonderbra campaign, to my mind an important reason for the merger has vanished. These things require a great deal more than logic to succeed. Trevor has been caught up in eight, poor chap, and as I write has failed to respond to Jo's lovelorn plea. He's had enough. I don't blame him, especially since if I read aright, the new agency has a crazy plan to share responsibilities among five creative directors. A grand recipe for chaos.

NOTE: Mr Beattie has since gone from strength to strength. So have Messrs Saatchi & Saatchi. Mergers and acquisitions are more popular than ever – and a recent one looks like costing someone called Hoare his job.

□ □ □

DATE: FEBRUARY 1997

WHEN ALL ELSE FAILS, WHY NOT ESTABLISH THE FACTS?

Introduction

One of my clients used to spend a prodigious amount of money every year sponsoring show-jumping. Their business was double-glazing.

I could never see what show-jumping and double-glazing had in common and I was not encouraged to ask. What I was encouraged to do – and thoroughly enjoyed – was attend show-jumping events, drink lots of champagne and meet the stars of the industry.

This sort of thing is the reason why marketers are not universally admired by their colleagues. If you compare the rigid discipline imposed on finance directors by the need to count the money and make sure there's enough left, or on lawyers by the need to keep the management out of jail, you can see why.

It is quite some years, for instance, since it was first learnt that promotions – various ingenious ways of giving away money – generally, if not always, are a complete waste. This does not stop most marketers from running them with great enthusiasm year after year.

Conversely, so few facts are known about other aspects of marketing that you would think the wise marketer would do something to establish some. Sponsorship is one. About 20 years ago I was hired by one of the world's largest firms to make a film about how motor-racing sponsorship was working for them.

I was quite surprised to learn that there was hardly any impartial information available. In fact I concluded that this enormously expensive activity was undertaken on two bases. One: somebody thought it would be a good idea. Two: many of their directors liked motor-racing and racing drivers.

Nobody ever tried to work out the difference between sales and profits without sponsorship and sales and profits with sponsorship. This is not as hard as it seems but it certainly was too difficult for that firm – and for that matter most firms today – to make a serious attempt to find out.

A NEAT IDEA FROM P & G

There is no greater evangelist for direct marketing than the US pundit, Stan Rapp. He 'co-authored' (to use that droll Americanism) the books *Maximarketing* (1987) and *The Great Marketing Turnaround* (1990), which I recommend. They contain much wisdom on how marketing should be integrated, and some particularly interesting information on the effective use of direct marketing for packaged goods.

A good example of current developments is a programme launched recently by Procter & Gamble in the United States, who are running a network TV campaign offering a money-back guarantee on Crest and Crest tartar-control toothpaste. The commercials feature a toll-free telephone number for consumers to find out more.

Many regard P & G as the world's best marketing organization. You know when they get seriously involved that direct has come of age.

Respondents receive a kit from P & G including an enrolment card. To fill out the card the respondent goes to the dentist who then rates the patient's dental condition. The card is returned to P & G, and for the next six months the participant uses Crest.

Five months after the enrolment P & G send a reminder to visit the dentist again. That reminder card is validated by the dentist after the visit. If the patient, or the patient's parent doesn't agree that Crest has performed as promised, P & G will refund the cost of six months of Crest – up to $15 worth, with proofs of purchase.

Some aesthetes in *Campaign* were complaining a while ago about how uncreative Procter & Gamble are. All I can say is that this idea is very imaginative indeed, and could do more for Crest than any number of clever ads.

The campaign is of particular interest to direct marketers, not merely for its ingenuity, but because it uses one of our oldest tools, the money-back guarantee, and because many regard P & G as the world's best marketing organization. You know when they get seriously involved that direct has come of age.

I wonder how carefully Procter & Gamble tested this programme in advance. It seems to me somewhat complicated. From a practical point of view, how many consumers will really go to the trouble of collecting proofs of purchase, for instance? Nevertheless, it is a very powerful idea, and I particularly like the way it involves not merely the customer, but the dentist – who obviously is somebody the company wants to get on their side.

Interestingly, in the same week that I read about that programme Texas Homecare in this country made an interesting offer. If you would buy a Wrighton kitchen, they would give you all your money back in 10 years. This is not a totally new idea – I mentioned a variation on it in the first edition of my book *Commonsense Direct Marketing* (1988) – but it is very clever because after 10 years how many people remember what they bought? And even if they do, you have had their money in your bank earning interest all that time.

I think Texas completely ruined this idea by putting in what looks very like a measly legal quibble: you are required to ask for your money back within a 28-day period after the end of the 10 years, and do so via a recorded delivery letter. To me this entirely destroys the generous impression the offer gives. In fact I suspect they have ended up doing more harm than good.

□ □ □

DATE: OCTOBER 1992

ECONOMICAL WITH THE TRUTH

I often quote *The Economist*: its air of lofty omniscience can be very persuasive. However I am careful only to quote it on matters of fact, because in matters of opinion too often it talks tripe – as the following extract from page 95 of the 27 April issue shows:

> As the morning post too often demonstrates, direct mail advertising is a sloppy business. Without much knowledge of people's likes and dislikes, advertisers resort to the shotgun approach. They send out lots of letters, hoping that some are opened, and maybe even a few read and responded to. It is grossly inefficient; the letters cost a fortune to send, waste time, consume a lot of trees.

Direct mail is measurable: you quickly learn to talk about benefits for the customer rather than about yourself or you go broke.

They should know. I have on file six *Economist* subscription letters all received in the same week by a colleague in Switzerland.

If the know-alls responsible for that example of prejudice masquerading as knowledge were to pause and think intelligently they might come to some sensible conclusions. For instance, why, if it is so sloppy, does their employer use direct mail to get the money to pay them to write such rubbish? The answer is that, even done badly, it works better than most alternatives.

And what about the poor trees? If they were to visit any British household and make two piles at the end of any week, one of all the unread or irrelevant ads the people in that house are exposed to in the press, and another of all the direct mail (about two mailings per average household) it would teach them a simple lesson. It might help if they also spent five minutes learning how databases work. They could then help save the planet by passing the knowledge on to their commercial brethren.

Of the 152-page issue which carried the piece quoted, 90 pages contained advertisements, almost all irrelevant to most readers, and where they were relevant often so ill prepared that those running them might just as well have taken their money and set fire to it on the sidewalk of some financial centre or another. No competent direct marketer would construct a piece based on the premise of an ad for Bankers Trust in that issue, which reads like an abbreviated version of a self-congratulatory after-dinner speech by the chairman. That's because direct mail is measurable: you quickly learn to talk about benefits for the customer rather than about yourself or you go broke.

In fact 28 pages of advertising in the issue were run by banks. They certainly wasted their money in most cases, since it featured a scaremongering piece about the possible collapse of the banking system. Would you run an ad surrounded by editorial suggesting your industry is a serious hazard to world economic health?

Yet despite the waste, *The Economist* works splendidly for one of my clients, just as direct mail works to get their subscribers. However, the piece in question was so sloppy that I must point out the truth, if only because – according to their mailings – the journal is read by ministers, heads of state, top businesspeople and other luminaries all over the world. I hope they don't take it too seriously.

NOTE: *The Economist* really seems to have got my goat. I refer to this example twice.

□   □   □

DATE: MAY 1996

HOW ABOUT ASKING YOUR CUSTOMERS?

Did you see the TV programme about the remarkable teacher Michel Thomas? He had children with little inclination or talent (one had been 'encouraged' by being told not to even bother trying) speaking French better in five days than ordinary teachers had managed in five years.

Great teachers are rare, incompetents and bullies more common. My first maths teacher, Geoffrey LaTrobe Foster – may he rot in hell – was a pig who made my life a misery. He imparted a loathing for the subject which only vanished after I learnt how intimately interwoven it was with making money in mail order.

> **Q**uestionnaire mailings to customers (which can get over 50 per cent response) would reveal many things, including their views on all sorts of things.

These reflections arose after receiving a well-written letter – itself a cause for joy – from Friends Provident suggesting a 'decent investment'. Compared to what? An indecent investment would do better. Paul Raymond owns half Soho and is the richest man in the country. But the letter explained that if I wish to invest in things that don't corrupt society or defile the environment they have a special fund. From that you might reasonably deduce that their ordinary funds are not so 'decent', from which it is but a small step to conclude that they're two-faced hypocrites. But, carping aside, the letter made me consider, *inter alia*, how better marketing could make them more money.

What have all the billowing clouds of waffle about Planet Earth (and that obscene politicians' romp in Rio) achieved? Even marketers who obligingly created 'green' products have been disappointed because, as we regularly rediscover, what people say and what they do often differ. Few people say they're dishonest – perish the thought; but many, when tempted to be, give way without a thought. Few people admit they don't give a toss about the environment, but happily some do care enough to do something as long as it involves no effort, which is why the mailing was a good idea.

That being said, some people care more about it than others, so before they mail all their customers Friends Provident should find out which. Questionnaire mailings to customers (which can get over 50 per cent response) would reveal many things, including their views on all sorts of things. They could offer their fund first to those who felt very strongly about the environment, then if that worked to those who felt less strongly, and so on.

This, for those who constantly bore us with the phrase but do nothing, is being 'customer-focused'. And goodness, how it pays. I have seen targeting messages in this way double response. A few years ago one firm, which took the trouble to ask how people felt about their motor insurance, claimed it made their expenditure work five times harder. Yet Friends Provident's disinterest in me is so total that I cannot recall them ever asking me anything about anything.

I offer these views in a spirit of public-spirited benevolence, bolstered by the sentimental thought that Friends Provident were once my clients. But a more practical reason is simple: I am a policyholder and wish they would market better. I'd like a bigger pension and a better environment to enjoy it in.

NOTE: The world's politicians had just spent disgusting amounts of money on one of their regular boondoggles to determine what should be done to help the environment. As usual, little was decided, less has been done, and a good time was had by all.

□ □ □

DATE: MAY 1997

IT TAKES TIME, BUT BUILDING A BRAND PAYS

To be honest, I'm still recovering from being patronized by Quentin Bell in the letters page a while ago in respect of my literary and intellectual pretensions. It felt like being advised on etiquette by a Millwall supporter. But enough of that; let's be serious.

The hardest job in advertising, I think, is the creative director's. Much harder than running an agency, I would say, having done both jobs simultaneously for a scary few months. Squeezing gems out of fractious, egotistical and childishly sensitive people is damn hard work.

Perhaps the best creative directors ever were Bernbach, Ogilvy and Burnett. In the United Kingdom, Stanhope Shelton of Mather & Crowther in the 1960s when they were the country's most outstanding agency and John Webster of BMP (trained by Shelton) seem to me superb exemplars.

> **If customers prefer your brand, you get more repeat purchases and they stay with you longer. This makes the long-term value of a customer greater to you, which in turn means you can afford to pay more to get and keep customers.**

Norman Berry, who did the job at O & M, New York in their glory years, was astonishingly good. Recently I re-read a 1987 piece by him in *Viewpoint*, the O & M house magazine. He discussed how to revitalize brands, telling a good story about identical television sets made in the UK under the names General Electric and Hitachi. Although the Hitachi cost a lot more, it outsold the General Electric model ten to one.

At a time when the average marketing director may wonder if he'll still be around next Wednesday, the long-term perspective required to build brands is in distinctly short supply. So perhaps it is worth reminding ourselves of all the happy consequences that flow from having a strong brand.

Norman's example – which is remarkable, but not unique – showed it can induce people to pay more for, and buy relatively more of, your brand. Another point he made which had never occurred to me was that a strong brand inspires trust, and even affection, so customers are willing to forgive your mistakes. I think they may even put up with an inferior product – sometimes the case with Microsoft products, in my view.

If customers prefer your brand, you get more repeat purchases and they stay with you longer. This makes the long-term value of a customer greater to you, which in turn means you can afford to pay more to get and keep customers. As a result, you can out-promote your competitor at every turn. If you make and sell more, economies of scale mean you can, if you wish, undercut and eventually kill the competition. If you sell the same number of items at a greater margin, or, even better, more products at a greater margin, as in the example Norman gave, you can outgun your competitor at every phase of business, starting with improving your product so as to strengthen your position even further.

I often read that brands are no longer as important as they were. I have never seen anything but opinion and anecdotal evidence to prove it, and the reasons for trying to build a brand remain as important now as ever. And since everyone is in such a tearing hurry to get results, I can only end with the Latin tag *'festina lente'* – make haste slowly.

NOTE: Quentin Bell, the public relations pundit, had loyally – and understandably – written a rude reply to an even ruder piece I had written about one of his more lucrative clients, a woman who in my view had blighted everything she ever touched.

□ □ □

DATE: AUGUST 1997

LARGE PROFITS FROM SMALL TESTS

I was once required at a conference, where as usual one was being asked impossible questions, to define the perfect client in three words. I replied: 'Willingness to test.' Many new entrants to the direct marketing field – the banks, the motor car companies and so forth – do not test enough.

It is the accountability of direct marketing which makes it attractive to many businesses. Whereas it is often difficult, if not impossible, to discern precisely what happened as the result of your advertising, with direct marketing you can track the effectiveness of various messages throughout the relationship with a given customer. You can see exactly what your money is achieving, and thus estimate accurately what you should invest to recruit and retain customers.

> **I have seen the addition of one word to a headline increase response by 20 per cent.**

The object of your direct marketing can be: to recruit more customers at a given cost, and thus increase the volume of trade; to lower the cost of recruiting customers, and thus increase the profitability of each customer; or to extend the period during which a customer stays with you, thus increasing the profitability of the relationship. You can only achieve such objectives by constant testing.

People do not test enough because they don't know how greatly small changes can improve results. One famous example was given by John Caples over 30 years ago, who reported that simply changing the headline of an advertisement had improved response by 19.5 times.

A few years ago my colleagues and I were able to cajole a client into testing a different letter in a mailing to recruit new customers for a credit card.

All the other elements in the package remained unchanged. But that letter (I wrote one over twice as long as the one then being run) improved response by 19 per cent.

I have seen the addition of one word to a headline increase response by 20 per cent, and other seemingly small elements can often have a surprising impact. I have seen a change in the colour of an envelope lift response by over 25 per cent, and in one recent spectacular example, a charity multiplied its response by a factor of 16, without changing the proposition, simply by switching from press to TV.

Generally, changes in targeting will make the greatest difference, but it's worth testing all important elements. In one programme for a client in the early 80s we tested six factors: list selection, offer, timing, price, creative and response method. In theory, if you combined all the best test results and compared them with a combination of the worst, you got 58 times more responses. I once showed this case history to a group of bankers in Salzburg. They knew little about marketing, but they understood money and were duly impressed.

If you are relatively new to direct marketing, I suggest you push your agency and your colleagues to suggest a constant flow of ideas for testing. This is one of the few areas in business where, for little extra cost, you can make a great deal of extra money. If you are not spending a good 10 per cent of your budget each year on testing, you certainly should be if you have an established business. And if you are a new marketer, the percentage should be much higher.

NOTE: Obviously the quality of your product or service is even more critical than the elements mentioned above.

□ □ □

DATE: OCTOBER 1992

LOYALTY, RESEARCH AND COURAGE

'Loyalty is what is left when the bribes are removed,' observed Victor Ross, former chairman of the *Readers' Digest*, Europe, in a speech a while ago in Spain. This pointed aphorism came to mind when I read a couple of recent pieces from either side of the Atlantic. One announced that Procter & Gamble in the United States plan to stop coupon promotions, the other that Esso over here has returned its Tiger points scheme to its cage.

Neither report suggested these schemes just don't work. P & G's decision was linked to a steep drop in coupon redemptions – from 7.7 billion to 5.8 billion in three years. Esso said research led to their decision, though

> I have never seen short copy making the same proposition as long copy pull nearly as well.

others believe that the growing competition from supermarkets means they just can't afford the scheme any more.

A client who organizes continuity programmes tells me that those that last more than a few months stop working. I hope to get some more facts from him on this, but his reaction to Esso's reliance on consumer research was the same as mine: howls of laughter.

As I observed the other week, research is often used to avoid making a decision for which one can be blamed. This would not be such a problem if a great many research findings were not either flawed or plain wrong. That's because people can often tell you more or less what they think but rarely what they will do, particularly when confronted by something they've never seen before. Moreover, they often lie – even to themselves – about their motives and behaviour.

Three famous advertising examples come to mind. When the Leo Burnett agency in Chicago planned to reposition Marlboro from being a ladies' brand and put tattooed cowboys in the ads, research said it wouldn't work. Someone who was there told me Leo was urged by all his colleagues not to run the campaign. Leo was not noted for his sly wit, but he replied: 'To hell with the research. We're running it – and if you don't agree, I'll go away and start my own agency.' I'm told the 'Heineken refreshes' and the surreal Benson & Hedges campaigns also researched badly. In both cases Frank Lowe, courageously, said go ahead.

I have never found anybody who admits to liking, let alone reading, *Readers' Digest* mailings – mailings which propelled the *Digest* into the pre-eminent position amongst the world's magazines as well as selling astonishing amounts of merchandise. Nor have I ever come across any research respondents who claimed to like reading long copy – yet I have never seen short copy making the same proposition as long copy pull nearly as well. And research invariably reveals that people don't read direct mail, which always makes it hard for me. How have I managed to prosper by writing things for which clients will only pay if prospects not only read, but also persevere right to the end and reply?

Research is no alternative to that rare ability to enter into the mind of the customer that some creative people possess, and an equally rare commodity: the judgement and guts to make and carry out tough decisions.

NOTE: I like that remark by Victor Ross so much that I see I have repeated it elsewhere.

☐ ☐ ☐

DATE: FEBRUARY 1996

REPETITION AND OTHER SUSPECT PRACTICES EXAMINED

In Victorian days young gentlemen were warned that, if they kept repeating certain low practices unmentionable in these respectable pages, they would go blind.

So far I only have to wear glasses, through which I recently read a very good piece in *Admap* on another nasty habit: the unbridled repetition of TV commercials. Recent research suggests that once your audience has had one chance to see a commercial in a week, hardly any additional benefit comes

> **R**esearch revealed that 30-second and even 15-second spots get you much more awareness for your money than 60-second spots.

from repeating it. I doubt this knowledge will affect many marketers, who cleave mindlessly to the gospel of domination and repetition. But it confirmed something most direct marketers already know: media are like fields, which after harvesting must be left fallow for a while.

Generally the first time a message runs you get the best response, because the best prospects reply first. The sooner you repeat, the greater the decline in response. In direct mail you have to wait six months before getting the same response from a list with the same message. Re-mail within a month and you get about half as much. In other media, other factors come into play. You can promote products of wide appeal more often than those of narrow appeal; the larger the space the less often you can repeat, while the larger a medium's circulation the more often you can do so.

There is good reason to doubt the wisdom of buying large spaces to gain 'impact' – whatever that is – or dominance. Doubling the size does not double readership or response by any means. If you assign the value of 100 to a full page, then assuming the copy remains the same, a half-page produces 68–70 replies or readers, a quarter-page about 48, and a double-page spread about 141. These figures have emerged, to within a couple of percentage points, in five separate research studies over the last 80 years. You may be wise, then, to have a space no larger than you need to convey your message in a way that makes it easy to read. Your agency may deny this, for obvious financial reasons, but it's true.

Some years ago there was a controversy in *Advertising Age* on a related subject: how long should a commercial be? Once again, research revealed that 30-second and even 15-second spots get you much more awareness for your money than 60-second spots. This again depends on how much you want to say. You don't need long spots to convey a simple branding message, but getting people to buy something takes time: that's why many direct response TV commercials are so long. To make people keen enough to buy immediately you must cover every benefit, overcome every objection.

Many of the great early advertising men knew these things, because they began their careers in mail order. The most talented of all, Claude Hopkins, who helped launch Quaker Oats, Pepsodent, Palmolive and other brands, based his ideas on what he earned selling off the page. Even today some leading exponents have had this valuable education: Dave Trott is one, I believe. In many ways the conventional advertiser still has much to learn from those who have to get results – or else get fired.

NOTE: Dave Trott – known as 'Trotty' – was briefly famous as one of the founders of the Gold, Greenlees, Trott advertising agency. He introduced what one might call a *Sun*-style approach to advertising with lines like 'Hello Tosh, got a Toshiba.'

□ □ □

DATE: NOVEMBER 1996

WHAT **ARE** THEY TALKING ABOUT?

It is often suggested (perhaps by those seeking to dramatize a dull life) that marketing is like warfare. It certainly has similarities, suggested by Field Marshal Montgomery's quip, 'World War II will end when the opposing sides have run out of paper.'

Most of the needless bumph marketers produce is due to two things: showing off and bad writing. People imagine long words and jargon will make them sound cleverer than they are and conceal their inability to write properly or think straight. The mundane is turned into the mystical. Thus an agency is hired to 'generate foot-fall into stores', that is get more people to come in. Or,

> **They feel marketers must establish their credentials by exchanging a few sentences of drivel, like dogs sniffing each other's arses to make friends.**

as an agency boss said recently, 'The phone is becoming ever more integrated into everybody's life.' This means people are using the phone more, but that's so boringly obvious it can't be made to sound important when said simply. Or someone is 'tasked' with doing something, rather than (more briefly) told or asked. People are 'proactive' rather than active; things are 'trialled', not tried or tested. 'Concepts' (not ideas) are new and innovative, not just new. You need 'core competencies', not skills or abilities.

Apart from wasting paper, this linguistic garbage encourages outsiders – and our colleagues – in their view that marketers are a bunch of pretentious tossers. And many entering this industry must be deeply confused and, yes, corrupted by the odd use of language – either strange new words, or old ones used in a peculiar fashion.

Some are so captivated that they end up talking in a manner quite impenetrable to normal people. They feel marketers must establish their credentials by exchanging a few sentences of drivel, like dogs sniffing each other's arses to make friends. For those of you in this unhappy predicament, I thought to provide a glossary of common usage, but I quail at the task, because some words can mean almost anything – and even contradictory things.

Take that sad duo 'strategic' and 'strategy'. 'Strategic' in people's titles could mean one of at least three things. Perhaps they've been moved sideways and given posh titles because no one knows what to do with them; or maybe they do modest but useful jobs not worth big salaries and can be fobbed off with grander titles, for example 'Strategic Media Planner'; or possibly someone really believes the words retain some meaning. This is impossible since they are now applied to any activity, however trivial, and hardly ever used in their original context of the long-term or important, but with how you do anything – like recruit new customers, write your headlines, or change your window displays.

If you wish to feel part of a self-obsessed community sitting in a sort of cabbalistic circle gabbling away to each other in a foreign language, by all means master this foolery. But if you wish to talk to customers or intelligent people not taken in by such balderdash, perfect your English. You'll be amazed how many of those who have done well (even in marketing) write it well.

□ □ □

DATE: NOVEMBER 1997

WHY NOT LOOK BEFORE YOU LEAP?

Last year I was dining in Sydney with an old colleague who quoted a line I loved: 'Direct marketing is the art of losing money in small amounts.' 'That's brilliant!' I cried. 'Who said it?' 'You did,' she responded.

I guess this proves if you spend all your time scribbling and rabbiting, you must occasionally produce a gem to shimmer amidst the dross. Even a stopped clock is right twice a day. Mind you, maybe I stole it from someone with real talent.

I remembered that little line when reflecting upon the recent Van den Bergh promotion that will cost the firm over three times what they forecast. In case you didn't read about it, they

> **We tested it against his cut-down version, which was half as long. The long version did 93 per cent better.**

expected about half a million respondents and a £1 million phone bill, but got 1.75 million replies with a bill to match. Whilst guffaws all round are in order, it's also worth asking why this happens. It can prove more costly than failure, as Hoover demonstrated.

Market research can't tell you what people will do, because they don't know themselves, but why on earth couldn't the Van den Berghers conduct a live pre-test before spending all their money and ending up with such an embarrassing success? The answer, I suspect, is that nobody suggested it. That's because hardly any sales promotion people understand the value of testing before you spend – just one reason why they tend to cock it up when they try to do direct marketing, in which testing is the bedrock. (Mind you, this ignorance is not restricted to them: it applies to other enthusiastic amateurs who think it's just a matter of 'doing a mail-out'.)

Let me give you the three reasons, besides ignorance and laziness, why people don't test. All are wrong. First, they suffer from the fond delusion that they can predict the future. They rarely can, as the Van den Bergh tale shows. Second, they think they don't have time. Third, there isn't enough money. Yet strangely enough I find that somehow they always manage to find oceans of time and money to sort the mess out later. I wonder how much of both those commodities it's going to take to deal with the consequences of the Van den Bergh imbroglio – quite apart from any irritation it may cause their customers.

Tests often produce astonishing results. The most famous example, perhaps, is a 1930s headline where a one-word change (from 'repair' to 'fix') multiplied response by nine. In the last two years I have been particularly surprised by two cases, both for the same client, a famous business school. In the first, a celebrated US marketing 'expert' – a professor, actually – was convinced my three-page letter to senior executives wouldn't work because they would be too busy to read it. So we tested it against his cut-down version, which was half as long. The long version did 93 per cent better.

In another case, I was featuring the face of the Associate Dean for Executive Education in all the ads, because I know people look at people. His colleagues objected, almost without exception – for reasons of petty jealousy, I suspect. When we reviewed the results – face versus no face – by an odd coincidence the difference was again over 90 per cent. In the end, we had to give everyone the option to have his or her face in the ad. But that's another story, more to do with managing human frailty than testing.

□ □ □

DATE: MAY 1996

236

WHY SHOULD THEY BE LOYAL TO YOU?

Introduction

Since business is made up of transactions – buying and selling or exchanging one thing for another – it is natural to conclude that the best way to measure success is on that basis. The more sales you can make for the least amount of money per sale, the better you are doing.

That is how marketers still tend to evaluate their results, though some look at it differently. Back in the 1950s Peter Drucker, one of the thinkers in business, suggested you should not just try to make sales but to make customers.

Other people latched on to this, including Theodore Levitt at the Harvard Business School, who said the aim of business should be to make and keep your customers. Then other questions arose, like how long you could keep customers, and what was it worth to do so.

Marketers are romantics at heart, so they began to talk in terms of loyalty and relationships. They began to think their customers had relationships with them, and were loyal to firms and brands, though as a former chairman of Marks & Spencer observed, customers are not loyal, nor should they be. Loyalty has to be won time and again.

Anyhow, you can be sure that whenever marketers start using such phrases, all sorts of sloppy thinking cannot be far behind. These pieces reflect that.

ANY FOREIGN BODIES IN YOUR DATABASE?

Mr Baldwin, prime minister of this country when I was born, reviled the press as having 'the prerogative of the harlot through the ages: power without responsibility'. And jolly good fun it is too, let me tell you.

I became a journalist at 19, after walking out of university because I was bored (more likely too stupid to appreciate the opportunity I had) and became assistant editor of a journal called *Cotton* – now long-dead, but relevant then because we still had a cotton industry. On reflection, since my youthful observations of the workings of the Manchester Cotton Board and similar bodies led me to predict the industry was doomed, maybe I wasn't that stupid. I used to write rude editorials about the US farm support policy, an asinine confection that I imagine inspired Europe's even dopier common agricultural policy.

> You can't eliminate wasteful messages unless you know exactly who your customers are... Individual data should eliminate junk.

A journalistic maxim states that fact is sacred, whereas comment is free. Often it is also wildly irrelevant, as in a piece I read some time ago on Tesco's Clubcard. The writer was critical of Tesco for spending about £50 million a year bribing customers to stay loyal (an investment which, judging by sales, has paid off splendidly). He judged their plan to use data gleaned at the checkout to target different categories with tailor-made promotions was silly because of the great advances in market research and the use of sample groups over the last 50 years. I don't know what these great advances are, but he said: 'You don't need to interview the whole country to find out what people think of Tony Blair. A sample of just a few thousand is usually deemed sufficient.'

This shows ignorance of the way marketing is going and of the benefit of holding data on individuals rather than groups. The fact that a percentage do or think this or that helps you devise offerings that will appeal to a greater proportion of customers rather than a lesser. But what if you want to talk to a small minority? You can't eliminate wasteful messages unless you know exactly who they are. Once you do you needn't waste a penny talking to the wrong people.

People tend to forget it, but junk is not confined to the postal system. There's junk food, junk television, junk advertising and junk promotions. And what is junk to me may be wonderful to you. To me Fairy Liquid commercials are junk not just because they make me want to throw up but also because I'm not interested in washing-up liquid. Despite this they have been successful for decades.

Individual data should eliminate junk. As always, though, theory is one thing, practice another. What you have just read was inspired by a letter a friend received from the good folk at Tesco. Impeccably addressed to her, it was in response to her complaint about a 'foreign body' in some vegetable rice mix she bought at their Rickmansworth store, and it thoughtfully enclosed £4 worth of vouchers in compensation.

This is more than kind of them, since she has never been anywhere near Rickmansworth for 30 years, let alone visited the Tesco there. Gripping stuff, this database marketing.

NOTE: What does it take for one of these loyalty schemes to succeed? First, you stand a much better chance if you're the first in your market to have one. Second, you must use the information gained intelligently. Tesco were first in their field and have tried hard to be intelligent – though, as you will see elsewhere, in one case they, or their data people, effortlessly changed one reader's sex.

□ □ □

DATE: MAY 1996

240

CONSEQUENCES OF A FREE RIDE

Even if there's no such thing as a free lunch there is such a thing as a free cab ride, as I have discovered to my delight. One recent Saturday morning I took a taxi to my London flat, and when he dropped me off, the driver said: 'There's no charge. This is free.'

Pausing to collect my senses – which were in considerable disarray, since besides being taken by surprise I had a colossal hangover – I asked, 'Free? This is wonderful. Why?' He said, 'Because this is my first fare.' I didn't understand exactly what he meant until he explained it was his very first fare on his very first day as a cabby.

> **You must make sure that the incentive you offer fits in with your brand.**

That simple gesture did more for the public relations activities of the London taxi driver than any amount of the usual flannel about how friendly, cheery and chatty they are. The truth is that their customer management can be highly unpredictable, unless you're a Japanese at Heathrow, in which case there's a fair chance you'll get the sort of bill you're used to when going from Narita airport to downtown Tokyo.

So let me repeat what I said at the time to Andy Demetris: 'Thanks very much, Andy, and good luck with your career.' I'm also prompted to make some observations about incentives and public relations.

Many people feel incentives damage their image or that those who respond to them are likely to be less valuable customers. Not necessarily so. Richard V Benson, who died recently, was perhaps the leading expert on marketing subscriptions in the United States. He affirmed that 'a subscription sold at half price over a period of not less than eight months will produce the same quality of customer as a full price subscription' – ie the renewal rate will be the same.

So if you are wondering whether you should try incentives, my advice is, do so by all means, but remember what Mr Benson was talking about. He was talking about an offer designed to **initiate** a relationship. Most incentives are simply deployed for short-term reasons to produce a quick injection of extra sales and make the marketing department look good, or at least half-way competent. Too few people do enough with the names generated.

Also remember that you must make sure that the incentive you offer fits in with your brand. Even a very pricey product will benefit from something appropriate. Six years ago, immediately after the Australian budget, Lexus put four financial experts in a studio and recorded their comments. These were edited overnight, put on a tape cassette and mailed to every Lexus owner in Australia, on the very sound premise that those who own Lexuses are more interested in money than most, because they have more of it to lose. This was a clever use of direct mail to effect good PR.

Even better PR was obtained, I think, by a car dealer in Queensland who used to write to people who had traded in their cars, enclosing a cheque for $50. The letter told them the dealer had got more than he expected for their old car, so this was a thank-you. Clever, or what?

□ □ □

DATE: SEPTEMBER 1996

DON'T CONFUSE BRIBERY WITH LOYALTY

Midnight yowls, pungent nappies, inexplicable tantrums: it's all coming back to haunt me. We have grandchildren.

I am besotted, of course. But not so much that I fail to look into how they are catered for, ie ways other people can take them off my hands. I was pleased, then, when one of my daughters told me Tesco had introduced crèches. That alone could win my custom. What's more, she told me, they have one of those cards that save you money.

> **V**ictor Ross suggested that 'loyalty is what is left when you remove the bribes'.

'They all have cards that save you money,' I replied, with the confident air of one who has spent some weeks advising a big retailer on loyalty schemes. 'I have the Sainsbury's one, and the Safeway one. The Safeway one gives you a 1 per cent discount the very next time you shop. I've got too many wretched cards in my wallet already. Give me a crèche any time.'

I have grave doubts about what most people call 'loyalty schemes'. I believe many will end badly – and maybe there is some linguistic justice in this, for the very word 'scheme' has connotations of trickery. The other day I was discussing the subject with a friend who helped to put together the American Express Rewards programme. I reminded him that one of their competitors – Diners' Card, I think – had a very similar programme some years ago. 'Imagine,' I said, 'what would happen if Diners' ever got their act together and produced a scheme with better rewards. Or what if Visa did? Barclaycard already offer a catalogue of gifts.' Luckily for American Express, Diners' have never shown even the slightest scintilla of marketing competence, and Visa in this country have terrific advertising but lousy direct marketing.

My doubts have been put into words exceedingly well by one of the wisest people I know, Victor Ross, erstwhile European chairman of the *Readers' Digest*, who made a marvellous speech on the subject in Spain last year. He implied that most marketers had not thought deeply enough about what loyalty is, or what produces it. He suggested that 'loyalty is what is left when you remove the bribes'.

And bribery is what most of these schemes are. Few attempt, even cursorily, to project any brand values. They are little more than extended promotions. Fine, if you're the first person to offer them, but very difficult to manage long-term. First others start doing it, and then everyone does it, and then people compete to offer bigger and bigger bribes. It happened with the newspapers in the 30s. It happened in the 60s with trading stamps. It's happened with the airlines. (And significantly, Pan Am, who were the pioneers, ended up bankrupt.) I certainly don't envy the supermarkets. As the *Sunday Times* reported a couple of weeks ago, they've already had to cut their margins radically in the last few years.

It all reminds me of the Anglo-Saxons (you remember them, don't you?). They used to give the Danes gold to stop raping and pillaging – it was called Danegeld. The Danes got greedier and greedier, until eventually the Anglo-Saxons just couldn't afford to pay the Danegeld any more. They had to stand and fight. All the bribes did was ruin the country whilst a tough decision was put off. There must be a lesson in there somewhere.

NOTE: I was talking complete piffle (not for the first time) in this piece about the crèches. They're offered by another store. But I stand by the rest of what I said.

□ □ □

DATE: AUGUST 1995

OLD IDEAS CHALLENGED

'Your composition is both good and original. Unfortunately the parts that are good are not original; and the parts that are original are not good,' said Dr Johnson to some poor writer. Few people think well and originally about marketing, but one is Professor Andrew Ehrenberg of South Bank University, whom I interviewed a while ago. In January he's conducting a seminar that should be well worth attending on consumer loyalty and response to price.

I've commented on his conclusions previously – for example, price-promoted brands are mostly bought by existing customers, so price-related promotions not only have no lasting effect, but also are merely a rather complicated way of throwing away money. But he has many other insights that, within the field he has largely concentrated on (fast-moving consumer goods in fairly static markets), challenge accepted ideas.

> Customers are mostly polygamous, not promiscuous: brand loyalty is a habit of buying one or more brands.

Thus, we may refer to 'our customers', but it seems these people are mostly other brands' customers who occasionally buy from you. In fact 'your' customers typically buy no more than 30 per cent of their requirements in the category from you. He questions the use of that word 'promiscuous', which has added a naughty frisson to so many dull meetings. Customers are mostly polygamous, not promiscuous: brand loyalty is a habit of buying one or more brands. The phrase 'strong brand' is misleading, he implies: brands are neither strong nor weak, just big or small. They differ in strength – if that is the word – because of their number of buyers, not their buyers' loyalty.

He strongly suggests the intimate relationship between customer and brand many marketers fondly dream of simply doesn't exist, because 'frequently bought' goods are mostly bought infrequently: in many cases about half the customers buy the brand only about once a year. And those apocalyptic changes in market share that make headlines – the Boddingtons and Tangos – don't reflect everyday reality for most marketers. Most market shares are pretty steady in the medium term. Despite all our efforts 'the dominant factor in brand switching is market share: brands of the same size tend to have much the same degree of loyalty'.

For me his most challenging statement answers the question: 'Are highly loyal buyers especially worth having?' He says no; generally a brand has few near 100 per cent loyal buyers and they don't buy it very much. This is a worry. I have for years advised my clients to use direct marketing to two categories of customers: those who buy most of the generic product, and those who mostly buy your brand. It seems to work for things like fragrances and booze. How does this square with his observations?

I also wish he would look more into areas like financial services, where there is little loyalty, but changing suppliers is such a pain that many people don't bother. Is there more to loyalty than sloth? In the car industry, which he has examined, buyers can be very loyal. With Toyota in Australia we found the repeat purchase rate was nearly 90 per cent, as opposed to the more 'normal' rate of around 50 per cent.

It's all a matter of having the right data, he tells me. I agree, and will ask him to elaborate when we meet again. Loyalty demands that this time I buy the lunch.

☐ ☐ ☐

DATE: NOVEMBER 1995

SUMMER DISLOYALTY PROGRAMMES

Goethe observed: 'With idiots even God himself is helpless.' This came to mind when at 5.45 pm one Saturday I answered the phone in my modest country residence to be greeted by a lady who said she represented Mercury. Would I like to hear about a new service of theirs?

There has been too much talk about loyalty lately – I have added my share of sceptical comment – but this has the earmarks of an intriguing new approach: a disloyalty programme. I was as polite to the lady as I could possibly manage; I felt sorry for her. None the less, this would be a good time for you and me, gentle reader, to ponder upon what strange process led some

> **The customer doesn't give a flying fart whether some wretched marketing 'initiative' is ongoing or not.**

nitwit at Mercury to think it wise to have innocent customers disturbed at home on a glorious summer evening in the serious belief that they want to talk about some trifling – and quite possibly useless – new service.

What could be more likely to make one think a firm had no understanding of its customers than this wanton intrusion? Whatever service they were selling, you can be sure it will be 'ongoing'. Shortly after the phone call, I picked up the latest load of old codswallop from British Telecom, all about their Business Connections. They send this bumph to me at home because nobody has had the intelligence to find out if it is my business address – which it obviously isn't. The mailing included a catalogue featuring a series of ludicrous conversations between models shot so as to make them look as silly as possible, asking embarrassingly ill-phrased questions like 'Can you tell me more about multimedia and the information super-highway?' Just the sort of thing one would naturally say to a BT operator – who would, just as naturally, trot out a witty riposte like 'BT can give you instant access to an almost infinite amount of information.' Huh?

On the back of the catalogue one operator informed me, 'We have a range of ongoing cost-saving schemes and special offers.' There is too much 'ongoing' going on nowadays for my liking. It is an expression used almost entirely without thought; 'basically' is another, and 'strategic' a third. The customer doesn't give a flying fart whether some wretched marketing 'initiative' is ongoing or not. Anything that is more than a one-off will go on as long as it works. Then it will stop. And nobody outside the marketing department will give a damn.

Another exhibit in my gallery of summer follies is from American Express, good friends of mine since 1978. 'Some time ago,' their letter said, 'you sent back your American Express Card', and then tried to wheedle me into having another. Fine, except that if anyone checked, they would know that though I did send back my personal card, I retained a corporate one – out of loyalty, perhaps, to a firm that has paid me a modest amount over the years, though if they keep sending me letters like that, my loyalty will be strained beyond repair. Why do so few marketers match their messages to the circumstance and the customer?

NOTE: Readers may find it hard to recall the name Mercury. This was a telephone firm who spent millions on a widely admired, award-winning campaign to establish their brand, unfortunately in the process neglecting to sell their services properly. They then had their name changed by the firm that owned them all along. This is what management calls strategy.

□ □ □

DATE: AUGUST 1996

THE DEVIL IS IN THE DETAILS

Here's the start of a letter from a widely admired marketer – part of their widely admired loyalty programme.

Dear Mr Nicholds

As a member of Tesco Baby Club, we'll make sure you're the first to know about new services for busy mums like yourself.

Frankly, you can't eliminate all such errors. Someone at American Express in New York once calculated there were over 100 steps to carrying out a direct mail campaign – ie over 100 chances to screw it up. I would urge any firm, particularly one relatively new to direct marketing, to ensure their people learn how vital the boring minutiae are,

> **A**merican Express... once calculated there were over 100 steps to carrying out a direct mail campaign – ie over 100 chances to screw it up.

because they can make you look really stupid. Arrange a few trips to see suppliers. Mistakes don't occur because they're all idle drones, but because many clients choose on price, not knowledge. So suppliers' bosses (who often make a fortune) pay staff poorly and don't train them adequately.

I'm grateful to Mr Nicholds for sending me the letter; indeed, I want to thank all of you who send in examples and write kind letters – and pray forgiveness from those I have been rude about. His unplanned sex change, though amusing, is not why I kept the letter. It shows Tesco are doing something intelligent with the data their loyalty programme produces. They are launching catalogues that are more likely to succeed because the data reveal, for example, which customers are best prospects for a children's catalogue.

If Sainsbury's are doing anything as smart I am not aware of it. I have belonged to Sainsbury's schemes at two separate stores since they began and have yet to receive anything from them – or if I have, I can't recall it. As recent figures show, most of the people who belong to these schemes don't even bother to redeem the points. Their attitude to joining is 'why not?' rather than 'yes, please'.

What Sainsbury's have going for them at the moment is little more than an updated Green Shield stamps programme. This may be worse than useless, because they are giving away money to gain loyalty whilst probably achieving the opposite. The customers who get the most points are the best customers. They are being trained to expect bribes in exchange for buying. So their loyalty is more likely to be eroded than strengthened. Perhaps it takes longer for the obvious to penetrate at Sainsbury's, but when it does, they certainly know how to get things done. When they set about launching their Reward Cards, the name collection effort was superbly executed.

But the names are just the beginning. In his history of the William Morris agency, Frank Rose noted that if you control the talent in show business, you control the business. Very true; but in marketing, the fact that you control the information doesn't mean you control the business. You must use that information. Those who use it best will triumph – in the supermarket or any other area. I'm just amazed that more people don't appreciate this simple point.

□ □ □

DATE: MAY 1998

WATCH YOUR WALLETS!

'An expert is someone from out of town who knows nothing about the subject, but has lots of slides.' A friend with Andersen Consulting told me that one.

I recalled it whilst chairing the Scottish Direct Marketing conference last year. As I love the sound of my own voice to the point of folly, I was wondering why I had agreed to do something that was unpaid and without the satisfying compensation of boring a captive audience.

However, the first speaker quickly gained my attention, not by what he said, which was both dull and hard to understand, but with the following definition of 'relationship marketing'. It was taken from the *McKinsey Quarterly* (1997):

> **T**esting shows what works and what doesn't; stops you wasting money; tells you where, when and how to invest it.

A marketing approach in which a company seeks to build close relationships with its current and potential customers in order to encourage them to concentrate a disproportionately high share of their value with it. The company pursues this objective by developing and continuously updating a deep understanding of each customer's present and future needs, and by tailoring the choice, delivery and communication of its value proposition to these needs as closely as is economically possible.

Such dreadful prose should be condemned for cruelty to English. More importantly, if I were a client it would worry the hell out of me, because if that definition is correct, relationship marketing is just direct marketing without balls.

I became an expert not because of my many slides, but because 15 years ago I wrote the first British book (Bird, 1982) to define direct marketing simply. There are three parts: acquiring people's names and putting them on a database, with relevant information; using that information to serve them better, thus retaining their business longer; and maximizing your profit by testing and measuring the results.

The third is perhaps most valuable. After all, in real relationships, the phrase that comes up very quickly is 'Do you love me?' followed by 'How **much** do you love me?' Testing shows what works and what doesn't; stops you wasting money; tells you where, when and how to invest it; and enables you to chart the progress of the relationship. It is not mentioned in that ill-drafted definition.

In Edinburgh one speaker said McKinsey have done over 100 database marketing projects already. Last month someone from a big direct marketing agency group told me his senior colleagues were spending more time worrying about the threat from management consultants than about their clients. Oddly enough, six years ago McKinsey asked me for my views on the future of marketing. Flattered, I agreed, and wrote a thoughtful document for them, which we then discussed in their grand New York offices. They didn't go so far as to pay me, but I thought I might use the story – 'Guess who the consultants consult when they want to know about marketing?'

These people are brilliant at dreaming up sexy theories that change every few years and selling them at outrageous prices. But often they know little about practice. That's why they're consultants. Direct marketing is intensely practical and detailed. Sales promotion and advertising agencies have been trying to do it properly – with little success – for 20-odd years. I can't imagine why these people should do any better, though the price of failure will surely be commensurate with their fees: far higher.

□ □ □

DATE: JANUARY 1998

WHAT DO YOU MEAN, 'LOYALTY'?

Can you resist articles about how much money people make? I can't. My deep-rooted insecurity always drives me to discover how I'm doing compared to other people. So much so that recently I was reading about Asian salaries in *World Executive's Digest*.

Despite frequent requests I'm not emigrating to Jakarta just yet; but in the same issue was a letter which I started reading because it came from Mary Carse, who used to work with me, and kept reading because she made so much sense. She is clearly biased: her firm runs loyalty programmes; but you may find a précis of her views valuable.

> Loyalty is not bought simply by offering rewards; it is earned by consistently delivering better value.

A rewards programme, she maintains, can only work as part of a loyalty management strategy. Many firms institute them, wrongly, as a quick fix. But loyalty is **not** bought simply by offering rewards; it is **earned** by consistently delivering better value. To do that your company's culture must be so customer-focused that you can guarantee to deliver the product or service promise **every time** and at **every point of** customer contact.

That has implications across your entire organization: from the staff reporting structure and how employees are trained, to the type of computer systems and procedures. Companies do not consider these crucial when they see a rewards programme as a marketing tool to deliver results in the short term. This leads to a me-too format, developed to get programmes going quickly regardless of how this may affect their existing operations.

Take some practical examples. How will points or miles be allocated, captured and communicated to the customer? How will redemptions be handled? These processes are not part of many firms' present structure, so they don't appreciate what skills you need to manage them. Moreover, many programmes fail to tailor the type of reward to the customer's status. For example, 'soft' rewards which focus on privileged service and recognition tend to become more important the more loyal a customer becomes, whereas 'hard' rewards like free flights are more important to first-time or infrequent customers.

Another feature of such programmes is that 'success' is measured by **volume** of membership rather than **value**. So money is wasted trying to convert persistent promiscuous users into loyal customers. This is particularly true where expensive statements and newsletters are mailed regularly to customers who haven't bought for long periods. Why not spend less on those people and use the money more sensibly by rewarding those most likely to become loyal?

Companies that do not understand that rewards are no substitute for consistently delivering value may actually create programmes that create more, not less, promiscuous customers. Such customers and prospects begin to **expect** an incentive to purchase or respond, thus diluting profit margins. They start to compare offers and buy depending on the best offer.

I agree entirely. I'm sceptical about these schemes; your competitor can always outbribe you. To me they are merely frills unless you are near perfect. Until then, invest your money in better service and communications. As a friend who runs the world's largest wine club observed: 'We sell service at a profit; it just happens to be delivered as grape juice in a glass.'

□ □ □

DATE: JUNE 1996

REFERENCES

Bird, D (1982) *Commonsense Direct Marketing*, Kogan Page, London

Bird, D (1997) *How to Write a Sales Letter that Sells*, Kogan Page, London

Caples, J (1983) *How to Make Your Advertising Make Money*, Prentice Hall, USA

Caples, J (1997) *Tested Advertising Methods*, 5th edn, Random House, USA

Jardine, L (1997) *Worldly Goods*, Papermac, USA

MacKay, H (1989) *Swim with the Sharks without being Eaten Alive*, Warner, USA

McKinsey Quarterly (1997), USA

Million Dollar Mailings (1992) Libey Publishing, USA

Ogilvy, D (1963) *Confessions*, Atheneum, New York

Ogilvy, D (1987) *Ogilvy on Advertising*, Random House, USA

O'Shea, J and Madigan, C (1997) *Dangerous Company*, Times Books, USA

Rapp, S (1987) *Maximarketing*, McGraw-Hill, USA

Rapp, S (1990) *The Great Marketing Turnaround*, Prentice Hall, USA

Rayfield, T (1992) *Dear Personalised*, JWT Direct, London

Roman, K and Maas, J (1976) *How to Advertise*, St Martin's Press, New York

Roman, K and Raphaelson, J (1992) *Writing that Works*, Harper Prism, New York

Watson, J (1993) *Creativity in Direct Marketing*, Institute of Direct Marketing, Teddington

Wheildon, C (1995) *Type and Layout*, Strathmoor Press, California

Wolfe, T (1999) *The Painted Word*, Bantam Books, USA

Young, J W (1988) *A Technique for Producing Ideas*, National Textbook Co., USA

Zeldin, T (1994) *An Intimate History of Humanity*, Minerva, USA

INDEX